THE COLORWORK BIBLE

*Techniques & Projects
for Colorful Knitting*

JESIE OSTERMILLER

Interweave®

An imprint of Penguin Random House LLC
penguinrandomhouse.com

Printed in China

10 9 8 7 6 5 4 3 2 1

ISBN 978-1-63250-665-8

Editorial Director *Kerry Bogert*
Editor *Nathalie Mornu*
Technical Editor *Therese Chynoweth*
Editorial Coordinator *Hayley DeBerard*
Art Director *Ashlee Wadeson*
Cover and Interior Designer *pnormandesigns*
Illustrations *Kathie Kelleher*
Charts and Schematics *Therese Chynoweth*

PHOTOGRAPHY
  Patterns *Harper Point Photography*
  Swatch lessons *Jesie Ostermiller*
  All other photos *George Boe*

STYLING
  Patterns *Tina Gill*
  All other photos *Nathalie Mornu*
  Hair/makeup *Valerie Salls*

contents /

introduction

COLORWORK WAS THE siren song that lured me into the knitting world. I had dabbled in different needle crafts when I was a kid, but what I really wanted to make as a young adult was a sweater with reindeer marching across the yoke. That meant colorwork! It all started with a quick introductory lesson and a kind friend who sent me on my way with two skeins of handspun wool and a beginners' knitting book from the 1960s that was packed with all the basic knowledge as well as some quirky monkey illustrations. Stranded knitting was the first colorwork technique I learned, and I have been in love ever since. This book is designed to teach you not only stranded knitting but also stripe, slip stitch, mosaic, intarsia, double knitting, and brioche techniques, each in its own chapter. To further encourage your colorwork confidence, you'll also find chapters on choosing colors and yarns for your various projects.

My educational background is in music. When learning a new technique on a musical instrument, you start with the most basic form of the technique and repeat it over and over again until it becomes muscle memory. Then you add just a little bit more and repeat the new sequence over and over. I wanted the techniques in this book to be presented in the same way. Each technique chapter has a small swatch lesson worked over a mere nineteen stitches. The lessons start with basic components (e.g., slipped stitches or yarnovers) and then evolve until you've learned the technique. You can repeat the rows for those basic components as many times as you'd like until you feel comfortable before moving on to the next step in the swatch lesson. Work through each technique by itself or string several together on the same swatch.

When you're ready to turn your new skills into actual knitwear, you'll definitely want to check out the twelve new patterns in this book. Every one of these designs became my favorite while I was working on it. I was smitten with the beautiful colors and snowflakes on the Highmore Vest and secretly vowed that it was my favorite, but then doubt crept into my mind as I draped the Saffron Shawl, with its sage green and neon yellow mosaic pattern, across my shoulders. I also thought maybe the Spark Sweater would be my one and only, with its speckled yarn and stranded motifs climbing down out of the yoke, but I can never say no to a winter hat with earflaps (especially a brioche one!), and so the Alpenglow Hat also became my favorite. I guess what I'm trying to say is, I have feelings for all of them and I hope you do, too!

My goal with these designs was to create a range of enticing pieces that incorporated all of the different colorwork techniques in this book. I wanted them to feel modern and updated but also like traditional knitwear. The silhouettes are familiar and simple, and well-suited to pretty much anyone. I hope they inspire you to try new colorwork techniques and maybe revisit some that you may have forgotten about.

happy knitting!

1

CHAPTER ONE

understanding color

COLOR MAKES THINGS look good! The right color combination can take a hat or sweater from a simple piece of clothing to an absolutely stunning, must-knit, must-have item.

Each person has his or her own preferences. You should choose colors that make you happy! But what if you can only decide on two colors for a four-color project? What do you do when you don't trust your judgment? How do you proceed when you start questioning yourself about what looks good? (We have all asked at least one of these questions at some time or other.) Luckily, there are basic tenets of color theory that make finding the answers to those questions easier. Understanding color theory will not magically guarantee you all the answers, but it will help you make some decisions.

In every knitting book about colorwork there's always a section about the color wheel and how to understand it. It can be tempting to flip past this chapter. What does it all mean? How can it actually help you as an everyday knitter just trying to create some pretty finished objects? This chapter will help you see how you can benefit from understanding the color wheel and how it correlates to your next trip to the local yarn store.

The Color Wheel

There are three primary colors: Red, Yellow, and Blue ❶. There are also three secondary colors that you get when the primary colors are mixed together: Orange (red + yellow), Green (yellow + blue), and Violet (red + blue) ❷.

When you mix a primary color with a secondary color, you get a tertiary color, like a red–violet or a blue–green. There are six of these ❸.

Altogether, these twelve colors make up the modern color wheel. Color theory is the study of how these colors relate to each other, depending on their position in the wheel.

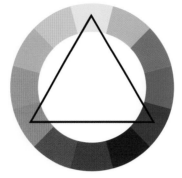

❶ *Primary colors*

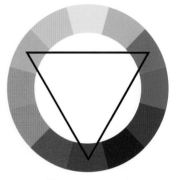

❷ *Secondary colors*

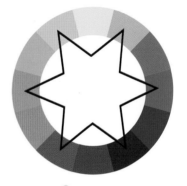

❸ *Tertiary colors*

The Lingo: Terms to Know

You've probably heard all of these terms before, but what do they mean? As you read this section, refer to ❹.

Hue: This term refers to the name of a color group (e.g., "red" or "blue").

Chroma: Chroma refers to all of the different versions of any given hue. For example, when we look at the "red" wedge on the color wheel, there are several different versions of red. All of them together are referred to as a chroma.

Saturation: This word is used in discussing how pure a color is. If you were to look at a line scale with black on one end and white on the other, a pure, fully saturated color would fall right in the middle. Look at ❺. If you start lightening a color by adding white to it, you create what is called a *tint*. If you move it to the black side of the scale you create a *shade* of that color. Adding gray to a pure color creates a *tone*.

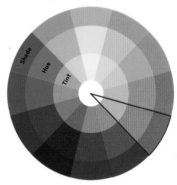

❹ *Chroma*

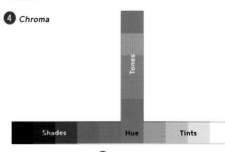

❺ *Saturation*

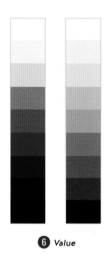

6 *Value*

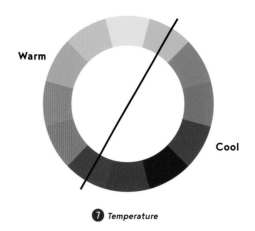

Warm

Cool

7 *Temperature*

8 *Complementary colors*

Value: Value refers to how any given color would look in gray scale **6**. This term is important in picking colors that contrast well together.

Harmony: A color harmony is simply a group of colors that "play well" together. Each grouping discussed later in this chapter can be classified as a color harmony.

Temperature: You can draw a line dividing the color wheel in half to show the "warm" colors (the reds, oranges, and yellows) on one side and the "cool" colors (the blues, purples, and greens) on the other **7**. The colors that this line intersects (red-violet and yellow-green) are welcome in both temperature groups.

How the Color Wheel Can Help You

Choosing colors for a colorwork project can feel a little bit like trial and error. The color wheel can't solve all of life's problems, but it can help us feel a bit less lost in the yarn store. You may have noticed that sometimes colors can look different depending on what they're paired with. Let's say you find a beautiful blue yarn that you simply *must* have in your next project. That blue can look completely different when you place it next to a dark purple yarn than it does lying next to a bright red. So what colors do you choose to go with it?

First of all, ask yourself how many colors you need for the design, then refer to these proven combinations/harmonies that work:

IF YOU WANT TWO COLORS

Try choosing from one of the following combinations for projects where you need two colors to go together.

Complementary colors: These are two colors that lie directly across from each other on the color wheel **8**. They will often give you high contrast.

+ *Pros:* Complementary colors offer the strongest contrast of all color schemes.

+ *Cons:* Even if you have complementary colors, they may still be too similar in value, losing the contrast effect altogether.

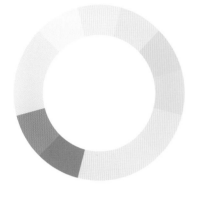

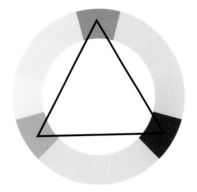

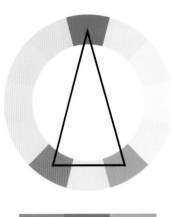

9 *Analagous colors*

10 *Triadic colors*

11 *Split complementary colors*

Analogous colors: These are two colors that lie next to each other on a color wheel **9**.

+ *Pros:* A good choice if you want a subtle, calm effect.

+ *Cons:* If the colors are too similar, they can get lost in each other.

IF YOU WANT THREE COLORS

Try choosing from one of the following combinations for projects where you need three colors to go together.

Triadic colors: These are three colors that form a perfect/equilateral triangle on the color wheel **10**, and they can also give you pretty high contrast.

+ *Pros:* Avoids the problem of having too much of the same thing.

+ *Cons:* These colors can look gaudy in combination.

Split complementary colors: On the color wheel, these are three colors that form an isosceles triangle **11**. This arrangement looks a little like the two-color complementary arrangement

above, but the first color gets matched up with the two colors on either side of its complementary color.

+ *Pros:* Not as dramatic as complementary colors, but still retains strong visual contrast.

+ *Cons:* This color combination can be challenging to balance effectively. The term balance implies equal parts. With a two-color scheme you can achieve balance by using equal amounts of both colors. When working with three or more colors, I suggest choosing one to act as the main, or dominant, color; then scale back the use of the other colors so that they become accents or supporting colors that balance out the main color.

Analogous colors: Exactly like the analogous colors described earlier, but with three of them lying beside each other in this case 12 .

+ *Pros:* Gives you the ease of a monochromatic color scheme but looks much richer! Also creates a calm and quiet effect.

+ *Cons:* Could be considered less vibrant because it lacks contrast.

Monochromatic colors: These are three colors in one chroma. In this harmony, instead of combining color along the outside of the color wheel, you play with combinations of the same color, varying the tint, shade, or tone of the color 13 .

+ *Pros:* This harmony always looks well-balanced and visually appealing.

+ *Cons:* It lacks the contrast inherent in complementary color schemes.

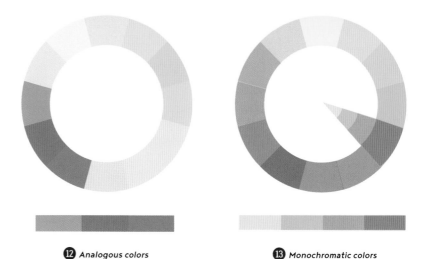

12 *Analogous colors*

13 *Monochromatic colors*

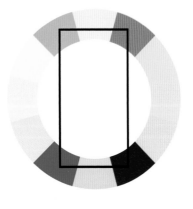

14 *Double complementary or tetradic colors*

IF YOU WANT FOUR COLORS (OR MORE)

Try this approach for projects where you need four or more colors to go together.

Double complementary or tetradic colors: These are four colors in a rectangular arrangement on the color wheel—basically the pairing of two complementary color pairs 14 .

+ *Pros:* Tetradic colors provide a really rich color scheme.

+ *Cons:* It can be pretty challenging to balance this many colors.

When choosing more than four colors, you could try using several analogous colors and their accompanying complements. Choose multiple tints, shades, or tones of colors to create blending effects.

Determining Color Value & Color Dominance

Let's say you've consulted the color wheel and chosen your yarns as best you could. How can you tell if they will look good together? Will there be enough contrast? Are they too similar to each other?

The best way to answer these questions is to look at color value. You'll want to evaluate the values of the colors you're considering using together to see if they will melt together or show strong contrast.

There are several ways to determine color value. You can use any of these methods with the yarn still in skeins or after you have knit up a swatch:

+ Some people can get a rough idea of value just by looking at a color combination and either squinting their eyes a bit or stepping back a couple of yards. This is tricky at best.

+ Twisting the yarns together can give you a fairly good indication of how they will cohabitate. Strong contrast can be determined if you can still see each color clearly the more you twist them together.

+ An easier and more reliable way is to take a picture of your yarns using the black-and-white filter on your smart phone or camera.  and  show the same photo, one in color, the other with the filter applied so the yarns appear in shades of gray. The further apart these shades of gray are, the better contrast you'll get in your design. You have to know what effect you're looking for when doing this exercise. The more similar they are, the more they'll melt together in a design and may end up virtually indistinguishable.

You should know—and take into consideration—the fact that some colors are dominant attention seekers while others play the role of wallflowers.

+ *Dominant colors* (aka "attention seekers"): Warm colors, light values, light or bright tints

+ *Recessive colors* (aka "wallflowers"): Cool colors, dark values, tones, and shades

Knowing which camp certain colors fall into can help you pick which ones to use in your knitting. Which part of the motif do you want to highlight and draw attention to? Where do you want the eyes drawn to? Use dominant colors in those areas.

Conclusion

As you work through the color techniques in this book you will have many opportunities to try out the information presented in this chapter. Trust your gut and use colors that you love, but remember the lessons learned from the color wheel and pair those beloved colors with other colors that will really help them shine. Since all of the projects in this book feature two or more colors, you should have no shortage of opportunities to practice color pairing. If you feel unsure about the yarns you're considering, remember to check their value (i.e., take a black-and-white photo). Try them out together in the swatching lessons. Decide which ones will act as the dominant colors and which will play supporting roles. Take the time to mess around with your colors until you find combinations that you love and that work well together.

tips for choosing color

It's time we all got a little more comfortable with color. Color can be infectious and delightful! Just think of the way a red scarf brightens up a dreary winter day, or how brightly colored mittens bring life to a tired fall jacket. We should be playing with color in a way that feels fun and lively, not intimidating.

We knitters are social creatures. We're like busy little bees buzzing around the most colorful yarns and snatching up new patterns to use them with. We see each other's projects in person or online and we can't help but be influenced by the color combinations and choices made. Instead of being overwhelmed by the options out there, view them as learning tools to decide what you like and what you don't. Take note of how knitters and designers are using colors in ways that you might not have thought of before. Don't feel confined to the colors suggested by a pattern, but instead choose color combinations that inspire you.

Here are some tips for picking colors:

✚ When in doubt, arrange your colors in rainbow order (remember "ROY-G-BIV" means Red, Orange, Yellow, Green, Blue, Indigo, and Violet). Rainbow color palettes are hugely popular in modern fabric lines as well as yarn lines! A fun way to do this color palette in a new, updated way is to either leave out one of the main color families of the order or to play with variations on the colors (e.g., hot pink in the place of red, or a rich mustard color in the place of a traditional yellow).

✚ Every once in a while, choose a color that feels out-of-the-box, or uncomfortable. Play with it, use it sparsely or heavily, and find out if it works for you. It might not, but you might surprise yourself. Often, a color that seems crazy can become more palatable when buddied up with a darker or more subdued color. For example, check out the almost neon-yellow shade used in the Saffron Shawl (page 140). See how it's toned down by the sage green pairing?

✚ If you feel like your chosen colors are dull and lifeless (which is usually because there isn't enough contrast), try varying the saturation of one or more colors (e.g., a lighter purple or a darker green) to bring more visual interest to the color scheme. You can also try making one color more dominant while using variations of the other colors as supporting accents.

✚ Swatch, swatch, swatch. The truest way to test a color combination is to actually knit with it. Start with the combination you think will work best, and then as you knit, if it seems like one or more of the colors doesn't quite work, you can replace it with another option and try that one out. Luckily there are lots of swatch lessons in this book to help you with this tip.

✚ When you really want a colorwork motif to stand out, go with high-contrast colors!

✚ Sometimes it is easiest to start with just one color that you feel strongly about. Once you have that first color, pick another in the same hue, but with a different level of saturation (i.e., go darker or lighter). Then find a complementary color that makes them really pop! Throw in a couple of neutrals and you have a team. You can see this put into practice on the Buffalo Plaid Cowl (page 122) and the Crossroads Mittens (page 104), where neutrals such as black, white, and gray are paired with one or more variations of the same color.

＋ Remember that colorwork doesn't have to be crazy colorful! Undyed, natural fibers are gorgeous and have an astounding range from dark to light. If you're more comfortable with neutrals, embrace that. Use saturated colors in restrained, minimal ways to pack a big punch. The Spark Sweater (page 144) is knit with two speckled yarns that read as overall neutral colors even though they're packed with multicolored speckles.

＋ Take photos of existing color combinations that you encounter and are drawn to, whether they occur in nature or in a bookstore or wherever. You can save images on your phone, online, or in a scrapbook.

＋ Be aware that you can have too much of a favorite thing. Most knitters tend to reach for colors they love and are comfortable with. This can lead to pulling a pile of all neutrals, naturals, or bright colors for a project. If you feel like your colors all fall into the same camp, try switching one out with its complement on the color wheel instead.

＋ Colors are best viewed on a neutral backdrop. When laying out colors to see how they play together, place them on a white or light gray background to see them at their best. The same idea can apply to bringing focus to a specific area of color on your knitwear. For example, a colorful yoke design like the one on the Yukon Jacket (shown here) will stand out much more vividly when paired with a neutral body.

I hope these tips will help encourage you to feel more confident in picking colors for your projects. Go forth and be colorful!

2

CHAPTER TWO

yarn choice

YES, IT MAKES A difference! This chapter takes a deeper look at how not only the color but also the fiber, texture, and weight of yarn affect colorwork projects. The previous chapter offered tips and information to help you choose stunning color combinations, but now you'll look at actual examples to see how different yarns play together.

Terms to Know

Let's start with a brief discussion on how we classify colored and/or multicolored yarns, just so we can all be on the same page. In recent years, yarn stores and markets have started overflowing with gorgeous hand-dyed yarns, speckled yarns, semisolids, tonals, and so many other color-rich yarns. Sometimes it can feel intimidating to figure out how to incorporate newer yarns or unfamiliar colors into your projects. By understanding what each of these labels mean, you might have a better idea of how to use them.

Terms like *fade, gradient,* and *ombré* all refer to different ways of changing from one color to another. Here are explanations for some of the different terms you'll come across. This is by no means an extensive list of what is out there, but a general overview of what's available.

Fade refers to a technique used to transition from one color to another (see the sidebar at right for more information).

Color blocking, on the other hand, implies a clean, abrupt change between colors, with no effort made to blend them together.

Gradient refers to a multicolored yarn that slowly changes from one color to another.

Ombré yarns also slowly change, but they stay within the same hue, shifting from light to dark or vice versa.

Variegated implies multiple colors within the same skein of yarn, with the color changes happening quickly or slowly.

Marled yarns are made up of multiple plies that are each a different color.

Semisolid or *tonal* yarns show slight variations of the same color as a result of applying dye by hand.

Speckled yarns are made by the dyer applying splatters of color onto a skein of yarn. The tiny dots of color can span the rainbow or be limited to just a few hues, depending on the personal preference of the dyer. Once knit up, a speckled yarn can often read as just one color even though it may be comprised of many.

So how do these yarns work in colorwork? For the most part, semisolid and tonal yarns (as well as some speckled yarns; see page 16) will act much like solids when used in colorwork projects. The bigger question mark involves the multicolored yarns and how to use them.

FADING 101

When you're planning fades, the main thing to remember is that you want to have a family of yarns/colors that can work together in harmony. Here are some tips to help you feel more confident in this super-fun and creative color blending technique:

➕ *Select yarns that have unifying characteristics. Look for similar base colors, or match the base color of one skein with the speckle color of the next skein.*

➕ *If the options feel overwhelming, try sticking with all warm or all cool colors.*

➕ *Speckled and variegated yarns will be easier to fade together than solids or tonals. This is thanks to all of the small dots that help create blended, overall colors.*

➕ *Placing the colors side by side is very helpful during the process of selection, but swatching with them is even better!*

Using Variegated Yarns

Let's look at how you might use a variegated yarn when it comes to colorwork.

The colors in variegated yarns can be beautiful, but they don't always combine well. Prior to knitting, the blue and the green yarns used to make the swatch in **1** seemed to be different enough on their own, but when used together with a stranded motif, the shared/similar colors make it difficult to see the pattern. If we replace the green variegated yarn with a high-contrasting solid (i.e., the white), as shown in **2**, the stranded design pops much more clearly.

The variegated pairing in **1** isn't entirely doomed. It might look okay with a different colorwork technique, such as brioche **3**, where there is no defined motif or pattern.

> **pro tip /** *For best results when choosing a variegated yarn for a colorwork project, pair it with a high-contrast solid in a color that does not appear in the variegated yarn. If you absolutely want to substitute a variegated yarn for a solid, select one in which all of the colors stick to either a color family (e.g., blues or greens) or a temperature grouping (only warm colors or only cool ones).*

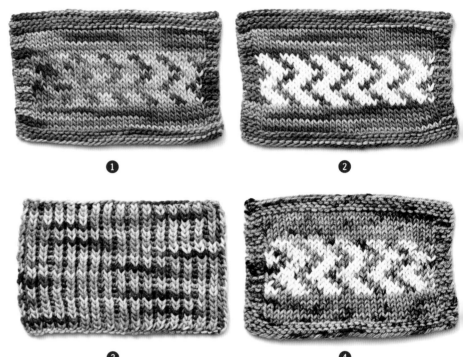

1 **2** **3** **4**

Using Speckles & Hand-Painted Yarns

A popular colorwork technique for using speckles and hand-painted yarns is two-color brioche knitting. These yarns really steal the show when featured in brioche patterns (you might try one with the Alpenglow Hat on page 94), but this is *not* the only way to use these beautiful skeins of yarn!

Speckled yarns, depending on the base colors, can behave like solids and create beautiful stranded, striped, and double-knit projects—and beyond. If the base colors of the yarn stay within a fairly close range (e.g., all dark colors, all light ones, all warm colors, etc.), then the skein as a whole will more or less read as one color from a distance. These skeins are perfect for colorwork knitting.

The dark gray and white yarns in **4** are both speckled and share similar colors, but from a distance they read as two contrasting solids.

> **pro tip /** *As with variegated yarns, you can replace the solid color of pretty much any colorwork project with a speckled or hand-painted yarn if it reads as a uniform color from afar (for an example of this, check out the Spark Sweater (page 144).*

Yarn Fiber

When it comes to working with different fibers, we knitters are super lucky to have such a variety available to us. Let's take a look at how fiber content might affect a colorwork project.

One of the first comparisons I think of is wool vs. cotton. Although the differences may be subtle, if you look closely you can see how in the wool example ❺, the fibers have filled out the empty spaces around each stitch to create a close, insulating fabric. This is because when wool is wet blocked (meaning that after being knitted it was soaked in water and then laid flat to dry), the fibers bloom and reach out into the empty spaces with their little barbs to stick to surrounding stitches.

The cotton stitches in ❻ are more crisp, with bits of extra space between them. This is because the fibers are naturally smoother and don't bloom like the wool stitches. This seemingly minor detail is very important to take into consideration with colorwork knitting. When you change colors in most techniques, you run the risk of creating small gaps between stitches (due to floats or the moving of the yarns). In many cases the colorwork knitter can rely on the blooming nature of wool to help smooth out the gaps and puckers in their fabric. This is why colorwork knitters have adopted the battle cry, "that will block itself right out!"

If you were to handle these finished swatches, you might notice another difference. The cotton fabric stretches easily but doesn't bounce back into shape like the wool does. As a result, garments and accessories knit in cotton yarns, although pretty, can lose their shape very easily over the course of a day or so.

❺

❻

pro tip / *Wool and wool-blend yarns tend to have the best texture for colorwork. Cotton, linen, and acrylic blends just don't serve as well. There are a lot of yarns that fall into more of a gray area (e.g., superwash wools, other natural fiber blends, etc.), so you should experiment and swatch with the yarns you choose. If you're happy with the resulting fabric, then go ahead and knit your project with it! These tips are meant to guide you toward colorwork success, but not limit you in any way or put restrictions on your creativity.*

Yarn Texture

Different textures can have quite different effects when incorporated into colorwork techniques. For example, a fuzzy mohair yarn added to a colorwork sweater may bring an ethereal quality to the design, tweedy yarns with colorful nubs can evoke rustic sentiments, and so forth. Here's a quick guide-of-sorts to help you navigate the many textures from which you might choose.

Worsted: This term can be used in several different ways, but here we'll focus on the word as it applies to yarn texture. A worsted-spun yarn is one in which all of the fibers have been straightened and laid next to each other to create smoothness before it's actually spun. The resulting yarn is usually very uniform and has a relatively firm twist to it. This results in crisply defined stitches that really pop in almost any colorwork technique.

Woolen: Woolen fibers are left to their wild ways and do not always lie down smoothly together, so when the fibers are spun into yarn, the result is a lightweight, fluffy, and almost aerated yarn that may also have a bit of a halo to it. These yarns are lovely and woolly and so fun to knit with, but they don't always create the crisply defined stitches that the worsted yarns do.

Novelty: This fairly broad blanket term encompasses any yarns that feature irregular or unusual texture (e.g., bouclé, chenille, chain, eyelash, etc.). Sometimes novelty yarns can be made of natural fibers, and other times they're man-made. Regardless of their composition, the question here is about how they perform in colorwork. The answer is "sometimes well, sometimes not." If you can combine a novelty yarn with a strong, stable base yarn, the effect is sometimes fun and exciting.

Let's look at some examples of different textures being used in colorwork techniques.

The differences in this first example are subtle but worth noting. In ❼, both of the yarns are worsted yarns, and you can see how crisp the gray stitches are that make up the motif. In ❽, the motif is just as visible, but the stitches themselves are just a bit softer and fuzzier because they were knit with a woolen-spun yarn.

pro tip / *If you want clearly defined stitches, choose a yarn that's more tightly spun, like a worsted-spun yarn. Using a woolen-spun yarn will yield softer stitches.*

Now, what if you really want to knit with a fun, textured yarn such as mohair or a novelty yarn?

In the swatch in ❾, the fuzzy, haloed yarn was held double and replaced a solid to knit the snowflake motif. It's a little messy, but you can still see the pattern. In ❿, a novelty yarn is used as a stripe. The irregular bumpy texture features beautifully when paired with a smooth worsted-spun yarn.

pro tip / *Novelty yarns can add a little extra pizzazz to knitting, but they also run the risk of mucking things up a bit. Use them sparingly for greatest success. If you have your heart set on one, consider using it as a stripe element or swatch with it until you find a way to use it in a different, successful, way.*

Yarn Weight

Does it matter what size yarn you choose for a colorwork project? No—not really—but different yarn weights can affect your projects in different ways. Even though the techniques will be the same, a stranded pullover worked in chunky yarn will turn out very differently than one worked in fingering yarn.

The chart below shows a basic breakdown of the most common yarn weights, as well as how they tend to perform when used in colorwork. The best yarn weights for colorwork appear in the cells with a pale blue background.

yarn weight	stitches per 4" (10 cm)	common names	effects on colorwork
#0 *lace*	33–40 sts	lace, cobweb, thread	*Stitches end up almost too small to see colorwork motifs. Intended for lacy, delicate items.*
#1 *superfine*	27–32 sts	light fingering, baby, sock	*Although heavier than #0, this is still intended for lace knitting, socks, shawls, etc. It can be used for colorwork but may be a bit tedious.*
#2 *fine*	23–26 sts	fingering, sport, baby, 3-ply	*Ideal for fine, detailed stranded colorwork and Fair Isle knitting.*
#3 *light*	21–24 sts	light worsted, DK	*Stitches are nicely sized and clearly showcase colorwork techniques. Fabrics created with this weight often have a very soft hand and nice drape to them.*
#4 *medium*	16–20 sts	worsted, 4-ply, aran *(this yarn is approximately twice the thickness of #2 or #3)*	*Great for garments and accessories. Knits up quickly with easy-to-see stitches. Larger stitches make it perfect for fast projects and very approachable for the beginning knitter.*
#5 *bulky*	12–15 sts	chunky *(this yarn is approximately twice the thickness of #4)*	*Ideal for outer-layer garments, chunky accessories and home decor. Fabric tends to be more stiff.*

ideal yarns for colorwork (#2 through #4)

HOW ABOUT A LITTLE DEMONSTRATION?

Each of the swatches on page 21 was knit from the same chart at right, using the intarsia technique but in different yarn weights.

The swatch knitted up in fingering weight **11** illustrates the point that small stitches can create more detail, and you can clearly see the relatively smooth line of the curve. A slightly heavier weight (shown in **12**) still produces a decent shape, but you can start to feel the choppiness of the knit stitches rounding the edges of the curves.

Bulky yarn, on the other hand, really emphasizes the shape of each knit stitch instead of creating the smooth line of the curve **13**. From a distance, the eye will still be tricked into seeing a smooth line, but up close we can see the jaggedness of the line. Don't discount colorwork done with chunky yarn, however. Using heavier-weight yarns can be a fun way to update traditional colorwork and traditional motifs. It's one of the hallmarks of modern knitting.

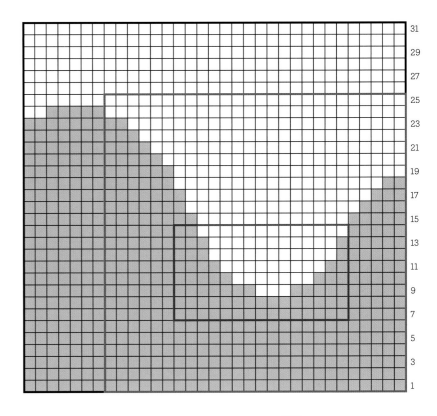

31
29
27
25
23
21
19
17
15
13
11
9
7
5
3
1

pro tip / *If your chosen project has lots of detailed motifs or curved lines, you'll find more success using a lighter- and medium-weight yarn. Using a heavier yarn can give your projects a more modern, pixelated quality.*

☐ fingering weight
☐ medium weight
☐ bulky weight

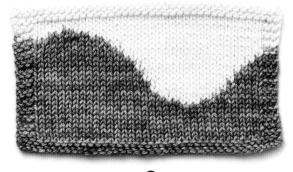

12

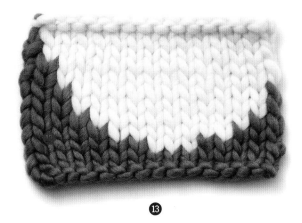

13

Conclusion

One of the most exciting things about yarn (and yarn stores and yarn websites) is the variety of colors, textures, fibers, and weights there are to play with. Ultimately I am going to tell you to work with what you love! However, sometimes we don't know what we love. I hope that the information in this book helps you to feel more prepared to embrace color and colorwork and feel empowered to enter a yarn store and be ready to experiment. Spend time swatching and combining and finding out what you love—and, more importantly, what you don't! By using colors that speak to you and that look fantastic together, you'll be able to enjoy the time *spent* knitting as much as your end result.

3

CHAPTER THREE
stripes

STRIPES ARE ONE of my favorite colorwork techniques. They look striking on sweaters, socks, hats, mittens, or shawls! They are a glorious first step into colorwork. Also, the possibilities are almost endless. Thick stripes? Thin stripes? A combination of both? You name it. They can be subtle or bold, decorative or strategic. Stripes can be used to blend two colors together and are amazingly handy when it comes to using up scraps of yarn. What's not to love?

This chapter will give you all the tools you need to successfully execute any striping pattern that a design could throw at you. We will look at carrying "resting" yarns, managing yarn tails, and working both flat fabric and in the round.

What You Need

For this technique you need only the yarn. However, there are a couple of things that will be helpful to know before beginning.

✦ You need to know how wide your stripes are going to be. This will help you decide whether or not you'll carry unused yarns with you as you go or cut them at each color change.

✦ You need to know the number of rows in each stripe. Although it may seem unrelated, this will help you decide what type of needles to work with. Although straight needles can be used for even-numbered row stripes, I recommend using circular needles so that you can knit any combination of stripes you might come across, an even or odd number of rows.

Attaching a New Color

There is no right or wrong way to attach a second color. The two most common methods are as follows.

METHOD 1

After inserting your right-hand needle tip into the next stitch, make a loop end with the new color of yarn (leaving a 3–4" [7.5–10 cm] tail) and slip the loop over the tip of the needle. Hold both ends of the new color while using your

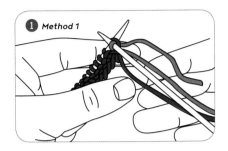

1 Method 1

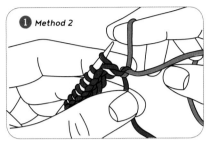

1 Method 2

right-hand needle to pull the top of the loop through **1**. After this first stitch, continue to knit normally. You'll weave in the end later.

METHOD 2

Simply tie the new color to the existing color **1** and start knitting with it.

Attaching a New Color Mid-Row

There are several ways to do this.

METHOD 1

This is my favorite method.

1 Work to the point of the new color joining, then place the new yarn (with the tail to the front) between the two needle tips **1**.

2 Pick up the color you've used up to this point and move it over the top of the new yarn, dropping it on the left **2**.

3 Now pick up your new yarn, insert your RH needle tip, and begin knitting with the new color. I like this method because the yarn tail can't be confused for a possible yarn source and it is properly interlocked from the beginning.

METHOD 2

Here, a slipknot joins the new color.

1 When you're ready to join the new color, make a slipknot with the tail of the new color and open it up large. Thread the ball of the old color through it **1**.

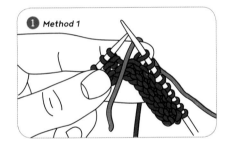

1 Method 1

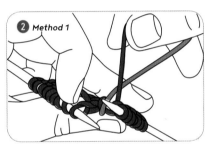

2 Method 1

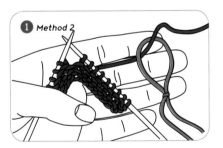

1 Method 2

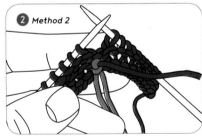

2 Method 2

2 Once threaded through, tighten up the slipknot and slide the knot down to the knitted fabric **2**. The new color is secured and can now be worked with.

After several rows have been knit, you can undo the slipknot and secure the end, making sure it is properly twisted around the other color. This method leaves the tail of the new color hanging on the back of the knitting.

METHOD 3

Insert your right needle tip, place a loop of the new color over the needle, and pull it through like a normal knit stitch. When it's time to weave in the ends for the color section, do it in a way that doesn't leave a hole next to the first stitch.

Chart-Reading Must-Knows

Usually you don't even encounter charts that are *just* for stripes. As with many of the other techniques in this book, each row of the chart will represent a row of knitting and will indicate which color to work that row with. New color stripes can begin on even- or odd-numbered rows, so pay attention to the chart.

Knitting Stripes in the Round

When you knit in the round you're essentially knitting a spiral construction. The beginning and the end of any given round never actually meet. Consequently, when you change colors in a stripe pattern you get a "jog" at the place where you make the change. (A jog is a small, visible step that shows exactly where the beginning and end of a round did not meet.) Personally, I don't mind jogs in my stripes. I like the physical reminder of where the "back" of my hat or cowl is. However, if the jog bothers you, there are several "tricks" you can use to disguise it. These methods work for stripes of any thickness, but are especially effective for stripes of three or more rows.

+ Important: For the following methods, the trick is worked on the *first stitch of the second round* of the new color. In other words, attach your new color, knit the first round of your stripe, then choose *one* of the following methods:

+ *Knit Below:* Insert your RH needle tip into the stitch below the first stitch of the second round, knit the stitch (together with the stitch directly above), then finish the round.

+ *Pick Up and Knit Together:* Pick up the right leg of the stitch below the first stitch of the second round, place the leg on the LH needle, and then knit it together with the first stitch of the round.

Moving your beginning-of-round one stitch to the left for every color-change row can help minimize the visibility of this trick.

+ *Slip-a-Stitch:* Slip the first stitch of the second round purlwise and then finish the round.

Stripes in Stockinette vs. Textured Stitch Patterns

Stockinette stripes have a very smooth, even appearance on the front of the fabric. When you flip it over you'll notice that the color changes aren't as crisp. What you see are purl bumps of previous colors showing up in the new color stripes, as shown in the photo at right.

This is because the characteristic bumps of the purl stitch are formed from the stitch found directly underneath it. This is helpful to know when working stripes of varying textures. To avoid "wrong color" purl bumps showing up on the first row of your new stripe, work the entire first row in stockinette (i.e., knit *all* stitches regardless of the stitch pattern). This first row of "knitted" stitches will be almost undetectable and will give you the crisp, clean color change characteristic of stockinette stripes. This is especially effective when changing color in ribbing, whether for hat brims, mitten cuffs, or sweaters.

Cut or Carry?

Whenever possible, I carry unused yarns up the side of my work. Not only does it cut down on the amount of finishing, but if you consistently pick up the new yarn from behind the old you can even create a sort of twist (or braid) up the selvedge edge that looks fairly nice.

When you begin a stripe of a new color, the old color remains at the selvedge edge of the work until it's needed again. If you'll be using it again within two to three rows, you can simply pick it back up, pulling up loosely along the side of the work before knitting with it again. If there will be more than three or four rows between uses, you should consider "tacking" or "locking" the yarn into the selvedge while working with the other color. If you don't tack it up alongside the work, the next time you go to use it you will be left with a long, hanging loop on the edge of your work.

So, how to tack? Simply twist the unused yarn around the working yarn and then let it hang at the edge while you knit with the other color. This keeps the yarn tacked to the edge every few rows until it is needed once again. (See the Swatch Lesson that starts on the next page for an example of tacking the unused color.)

If you choose to cut each color instead of carrying it along, be aware that sooner or later you'll have to deal with all the ends. Whether you weave them in as you go or all at once at the end of the project doesn't really matter much. Do whatever works for you! However, you must know that it's also acceptable to never weave the ends in and call them purposeful, decorative fringe. If you choose to cut, leave yourself 6–8" (15–20.5 cm) long tails for weaving in.

Even and Odd Stripes

For many years I assumed that when working flat you could only knit stripes with an even number of rows (2, 4, 6, etc.). This is simply not true! There are, however, a couple of rules that apply when working flat with an even or odd number of rows.

Even-row stripes: These are the easiest type of stripes to knit, because the yarn is always left and picked up on the same side, accessible and ready when you need it.

Odd-row stripes: When you're working with odd numbers of rows (1, 3, 5, etc.), you will need to use a needle with two tips (i.e., circular or double-pointed) to execute the "slide" technique. After completing a stripe and leaving your yarn hanging at the edge you will notice that your next color is hanging out waiting for you on the *other* side of your work. The way to reach it is by sliding all of your stitches to the opposite end of your needles and picking it up to work. (See the Swatch Lesson for an example of the slide technique.)

These rules apply to flat knitting only. When you're knitting in the round these stripe rules do *not* apply, since the beginning and end of every round occur at the same point. Your main consideration when working in the round is when to tack in unused colors.

continued on page 28 »

SWATCH LESSON

THIS LESSON WILL give you practice with even and odd stripes, tacking in unused yarn, and how to start a textured-stitch stripe. As you work, you'll refer to the chart below.

✚ **Note:** *Feel free to repeat any of the rows as many times as you'd like so that you feel comfortable with the techniques before moving on.*

Using the darker yarn and a circular or dpn, cast on 19 sts (or, since each swatch lesson in this book uses 19 sts, continue working on a previously made swatch left over from another chapter). Knit 3 rows to create a garter stitch border that will not roll.

Rows 1–4: You'll start with 2-row stripes, which are the easiest to manage because the working yarn is always in the same position at the right side of the work. Knit 1 row, then turn and purl back **1**. Next, attach a lighter color using your preferred method and knit 1 row, then turn and purl back **2**.

Rows 5–10: Once you're comfortable knitting 2-row stripes, increase the row count but keep it an even number. After working 4 rows, tack the unused color into the side of the selvedge by twisting the 2 yarns around each other until the unused yarn is trapped inside of the working yarn **3**, then work 2 more rows.

4 shows what the wrong side looks like after completing the 6-row stripe with the tack. How often you tack in unused yarns is personal preference, but I suggest not letting them float more than 4 rows.

Rows 11–14: Next you'll practice stripes with odd numbers of rows (1, 3, 5, etc.), beginning with single-row stripes. With the light color, knit across the row and leave the yarn hanging on the left side.

Slide your knitting to the other end of your circular needle (this is why you need a needle with a tip on each end!) and pick up the darker color to work a single-row stripe **5**.

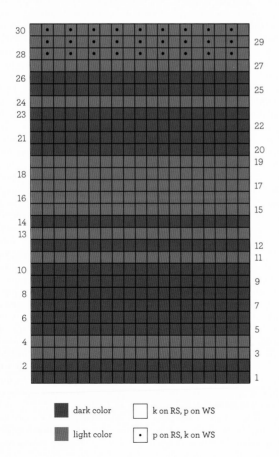

the finished swatch

■ dark color	☐ k on RS, p on WS
■ light color	⊡ p on RS, k on WS

With the row finished, you now have both colors on the left-hand side of the work and are ready to turn and purl back, starting with the lighter color, then sliding the stitches back to the other end to work the darker color.

After purling back with both colors, your ends will be on the right side again .

Rows 15–19: Let's increase the row count to a larger odd number and practice tacking our unused yarn, first on the right side and then on the left side of the work. Use the lighter yarn to work 4 rows and tack in the unused color before the fifth row. Knit across the fifth row of the stripe and leave the light color on the left side . Slide your stitches to the other end to work the dark color. At the end of the third row you will be on the left side of the work (where your light color is waiting). You will tack in the unused color in the same way on the purl row, by twisting it around the working yarn. Purl back with the dark color. To bring both colors back to the same side, slide your work to the other end of the needle and purl back with the lighter color as well.

The last thing to practice is changing stitch patterns in subsequent stripes. First work Rows 25 and 26, a 2-row stripe of the dark color.

Rows 27–30: We want our next stripe to be worked in k1, p1 rib. To disguise the purl bumps that would normally appear in that first row of texture, knit *all* the stitches in the first row and then begin the ribbing on the second row. Here, I've only worked 2 rows and you can already start to see that the first row of knit stitches is beginning to "disappear" and not be noticeable .

Working a few more rows of the ribbing pattern shows that the initial knit row

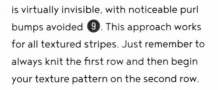

is virtually invisible, with noticeable purl bumps avoided . This approach works for all textured stripes. Just remember to always knit the first row and then begin your texture pattern on the second row.

BO all stitches or leave them live to practice another colorwork technique.

>> continued from page 25

Fibonacci Sequences

You can't have a chapter about stripes without mentioning the Fibonacci sequence. A recurring theme in nature, this sequence of numbers is built by adding each number to the one that came right before it, starting with 0 and 1. (Refer to the box at the bottom of this column to see the beginning of the sequence. The sequence continues on ad infinitum, but for the purposes of knitting we usually don't work in stripes of more than 13 rows.)

Why would this be of interest to a knitter? Besides being pleasing to the eye, this sequence of numbers provides a perfect formula for blending two colors together. If you knit stripes using the numbers of rows that appear consecutively in the Fibonacci series, with the colors going in opposite directions, the overall effect is a perfect blend of the two colors. Stick with me, this sounds complex in written form, but is very simple in reality!

Look at the top left grid on page 29. If you had 12 rows to work with, you would introduce color B by knitting rows starting on the small end of the Fibonacci order and knitting in progressively larger numbers (1 row, 2 rows, 3 rows), while the color you're

fading out—A—is worked in reverse order (3, 2, 1), so the entire sequence is as follows: 1 row of color B, 3 rows of color A, 2 rows of color B, 2 rows of color A, 3 rows of color B, then 1 last row of color A before knitting solely with color B.

This will work over 22 rows (using stripes of 1, 2, 3, and 5) or 38 rows (stripes of 1, 2, 3, 5, and 8)—as also shown on page 29—or more rows, depending on the size of your project and the number of rows available to work with.

Helpful Hints

Disguising jogs in the round: When trying to disguise jogs with striping in the round, use yarns that are not slippery or superwash. A yarn that has a bit more natural fiber fuzz (or tooth) is more forgiving and will make it easier to hide the jog.

Diagonal stripes: Work them using either the stranded colorwork technique (found in Chapter Four) or on the bias by knitting flat back and forth and using increases and decreases to create the shape of your fabric.

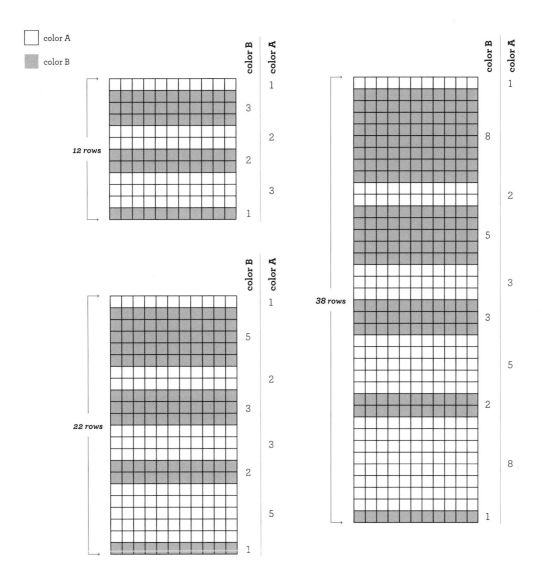

color A

color B

color B | color A
12 rows
1
3
2
2
3
1

color B | color A
22 rows
1
5
2
3
3
2
5
1

color B | color A
38 rows
1
8
2
5
3
3
5
2
8
1

✦ **Example:** To knit a square of diagonal stripes, you will literally tip the square onto its side to work in a diamond shape, and start at the lower point with only 2 or 3 stitches. You will increase 1 stitch at the beginning of each row (or 1 stitch on each side, if you want to keep the increases on the same row) until you reach your desired width. Then you will work decreases in the same manner until you are back to 2–3 stitches and bind off.

Maintaining tension: When you pick up a color that hasn't been used for a few rows, give it a gentle tug to help firm up the last stitch that it was used to make. Look at the stitch from the right side and pull the yarn just enough to help it match the stitches surrounding it, nice and even.

Tacking multiple times: In the swatch lesson, you practiced tacking an unused yarn only once during a stripe. However, if you wish to carry the unused yarn and are working through a deeper stripe, or with multiple colors, you will need to tack in the unused yarns 2 or more times in a row. I suggest tacking an unused yarn at least every 4 rows.

4

CHAPTER FOUR

stranded

STRANDED KNITTING IS the first colorwork technique I tried and will always be my first love. Striking and attention-grabbing, it's simpler to work than it appears. With stranded knitting you work with two colors at once, alternating them to create pictures and designs. Whichever color you're not using gets "stranded" across the back of the fabric until it's needed again—hence the name. These strands, aka floats, create a warm, two-layer fabric ideal for sweaters, hats, mittens, etc.

The term Fair Isle knitting often gets used synonymously with stranded knitting. However, it's more accurate to define it as a type of stranded knitting, originating from the Shetland Islands and having its own unique characteristics. Other types of stranded knitting include Nordic, Scandinavian, Icelandic, and more.

Traditionally, stranded knitting designs have consisted of frequent color changes and simple, geometric motifs easy to commit to memory. Modern designs often have longer sections of one color (requiring the knitter to secure long floats) and any number of variations on motifs, geometric and otherwise.

What You Need

To successfully work a stranded knitting project, there are a few things you should consider.

Yarn choice: Your choice of yarn will greatly influence the finished product. I recommend using wool yarn (or wool blends), because it's a rather forgiving fiber that can be coaxed and shaped with the help of water or steam, allowing you to fix any small bumps and uneven areas in the work. Cotton or acrylic fibers are less willing to be reshaped. It's also worth noting that if you're looking for significant stitch definition, you'll want to choose a yarn with more plies (think worsted spun) instead of a looser-spun yarn. (For examples, see Chapter Two, pages 17–18).

Gadgets: If you knit with two colors in one hand, it can be helpful to wear a yarn guide (also known as a knitting thimble or a yarn stranding guide) over your index fingertip to keep the strands separate while you work. There are several varieties available for you to experiment with.

larger repeats, you may find it helpful to place stitch markers on your needles, separating each repeat and making it easier to keep track of where you are on the chart.

For more tips on reading charts, see the Helpful Hints on page 39.

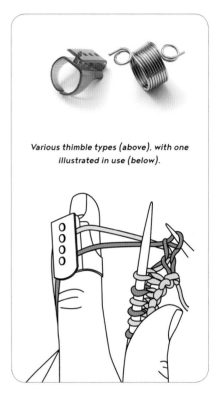

Various thimble types (above), with one illustrated in use (below).

Chart-Reading Must-Knows

Stranded knitting charts are pictorial representations of the stitches in your knitting. Each square represents a stitch in your fabric, as seen from the right side. Charts are read horizontally, from right to left (because that's the natural direction you work your stitches). (The exception to this rule is knitting a flat piece, in which case your wrong-side [WS] rows will be read from left to right. If wrong-side rows are not labeled on the left side of the chart, it may be helpful to draw directional arrows on each row to help you remember what direction you will be working.) Charts are also read from bottom to top (because knitting is worked row upon row). Charts are accompanied by keys that tell you how stitches are to be worked and in what color. If a chart is printed in only black and white, the different colors will usually be represented by symbols.

REPEATS

An area of the chart that is meant to be repeated multiple times is usually surrounded by bold or colored lines. If there are extra stitches on the outside of the repeat lines, these stitches get worked only once in a row/round. When working

How to Hold the Yarn

There's no way around it: holding two yarns at once takes practice. However, if you invest the time you'll be rewarded with even stitches, enviable tension, and gorgeous finished projects.

There are millions of knitters in the world and almost as many ways to hold the yarn. The right way is whatever way works best for you, end of story. If you don't yet know what works best for you, this chapter will show you several methods to try and you can decide for yourself.

You'll find various styles of stitch markers in yarn and craft stores.

There are three basic options, all illustrated at the right.

You can hold one color in each hand ①. This is known as Combined style, and is my preferred method.

Or you may hold both colors in the left hand, both strands coming over your index finger ②. Splitting up the yarns, with one over the index and one over the middle finger, may be easier for you. Either way, this is known as Continental style.

Or hold both colors in the right hand, either with both colors over the same finger ③ or split with one on the index and one on the middle finger. This is called English or American style.

I prefer one in each hand because you don't have to reposition the yarns as often, since you're never dropping the unused color and never having to re-tension a yarn, and you can work with both colors regardless of whether they're used in equal amounts or not. If you hold both colors in one hand and use them in unequal amounts, one strand will eventually get looser than the other and you'll end up stopping frequently to reposition and re-tension the yarns.

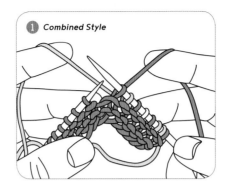

① Combined Style

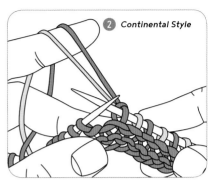

② Continental Style

③ English or American Style

The dominant color comes from underneath the nondominant color on the back of the work, and since you're pulling the yarn up from underneath it tends to create a slightly larger stitch. The nondominant color coming from the top creates a smaller stitch. The difference is minimal but over the course of a larger project can usually be seen quite clearly.

Taking these facts into consideration, you might see why it's important for each color to maintain its position. Switching them around midway through a project can create a different look even when using the same pattern. If you're knitting a pair of socks or mittens, you'll want to maintain the same color positions for both items.

It's better to err toward having floats that are too long/too loose, as these can be doctored a bit and "saved." Floats that are too short or too tight cannot. The key to getting a perfectly tensioned float is taking the time to look at the stitches on your right-hand needle. When you pick up the color that you haven't been using, make sure you spread out the stitches that this unused color will have to span before knitting with it. If the right-hand stitches are too bunched up, your float will be too tight. Spread them out evenly until they match the tension of the rest of your fabric and then create your float.

Yarn Dominance

Now that we've talked about how to hold the yarn, the next question is which color goes where. Regardless of how you hold your yarn, you'll have a color that lies to the left and one that lies to the right. The key to beautiful colorwork is keeping these colors in the same position throughout your work. Typically your pattern color (referred to as *dominant*) is held on the left and your background color (*nondominant*) is held on the right.

Floats

Let's talk about floats (or strands, or carries — they all mean the same thing). These are the little loops of unused yarn that lie on the wrong side of your fabric. If they're too short, your fabric puckers and folds. If they're too long, your stitches will be floppy and misshapen. These are common problems that will gradually disappear with practice.

Trapping Floats

There are floats and then there are "superfloats." Superfloats will catch your fingers when found in mittens and sleeves and are annoying! To get rid of them you must "trap" them to the wrong side of the fabric.

The simplest way is to twist the two colors around each other to make sure the unused color stays close to the fabric.

However, this creates a crazy tangle that might end your relationship with stranded knitting. Instead, try the following techniques. They may seem complicated at first but will make you feel like a knitting wizard once you master them. The basic idea is that the yarn you're trying to trap "gets in the way" of the next stitch and then quickly "gets out of the way" before

the stitch is completed, getting trapped behind the work.

This is done differently depending on how you hold your yarn; just follow the instructions for the method you use to hold your yarn. They're given in relation to which yarn color you wish to trap, the right or the left. Insert the right needle tip into the next stitch as if to knit and then follow the steps described.

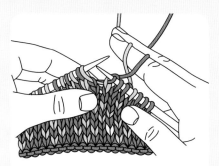

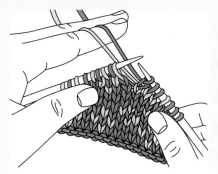

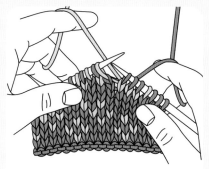

For English:
Both Colors in Right Hand

Trap right color: *Wrap the right color counterclockwise around the needle tip as if to knit, then wrap the left color in the same direction. Now unwrap the right color and complete the stitch with the left color. To complete the trap, knit one additional stitch with the left color.*

Trap left color: *Wrap the left color clockwise around the needle tip (this will feel strange, but it keeps your resulting stitch oriented correctly), then wrap the right color around the tip counterclockwise. Now unwrap the left color and complete the stitch with the right color. To complete the trap, knit one additional stitch with the right color.*

For Continental:
Both Colors in Left Hand

Trap right color: *Reach your needle tip over and behind both colors. Come under the right color to pick up the left color and bring it back the way you came, using it to complete the stitch. To complete the trap, knit one additional stitch with the left color.*

Trap left color: *Reach under both colors to pick up the right color. Bring it back under to complete the stitch. Knit the next stitch by reaching over both colors to pick up the right color, completing the trap.*

For Combined:
One Color in Each Hand

Trap right color: *Wrap the right color counterclockwise around the needle tip as if to knit, then wrap the left color in the same direction. Now unwrap the right color and complete the stitch with the left color.*

Trap left color: *Bring the left color over the top of the right needle tip counterclockwise, (resting it in the V created by the needle tips). Wrap the right color around counterclockwise. Move the left color back out of the way and complete the stitch with the right color. To complete the trap, knit one additional stitch with the right color.*

+ **Important note for all methods:** *As a final step before continuing, check the float on the wrong side to make sure it's not too tight or too loose, and to make sure it didn't pull through to the front when trapped. For more info, see "Traps showing through?" in the Helpful Hints on page 39.*

TRAPPING FLOATS WHILE PURLING

It may seem tricky at first, but the idea is basically the same when working on the wrong side of the fabric.

Trap right color: Wrap the right color clockwise around the needle tip, wrap the left color counterclockwise, and then unwrap the right color. Purl one more stitch.

Trap left color: Bring the left color in front of the needle just enough so it's in the way. Wrap the right color counterclockwise, then move the left color back out of the way. Purl one more stitch.

Weaving In Ends

Stranded knitting tends to generate a lot of yarn ends that you'll want to take care of at some point. I usually alternate between the two following methods for handling my yarn ends.

As you go: You can weave in ends as you knit by "trapping" the yarn tail on every other stitch or wrapping the yarn tail around the working yarn until it runs out. When you introduce a new color, you can start trapping the tail in 1–2" (2.5–5 cm) early before the color is first used.

At the end: Use a crochet hook or blunt needle to thread the yarn tail through the backs of the stitches, and then double back a couple of stitches and pull the yarn tail through itself before trimming it short. If you're dealing with an end that's on the short side, you can always put the tip of the needle through the stitches first and then thread the yarn tail through the needle eye and pull it all the way through the stitches.

✦ *Note: You can also just tie the ends together, a common practice in traditional Shetland knitting.*

Blocking

Colorwork knitting *loves* to be blocked. There are two main ways to block your knitting:

✦ *Wet blocking:* entirely immersing your knitting in water

✦ *Steam blocking:* coaxing the fibers into shape using only steam

For colorwork knitting I always choose to wet block. Colorwork truly shines once it has been dunked in water, pinned out, and dried. When the fibers go into the bath, they soak up water and bloom, magically easing the stitches into place. Unfortunately, blocking can't solve all your problems, but it *can* make a huge difference in how your finished project looks.

Here's what I think is the best way to wet block. Place the knitting in the water, making sure the fibers get nice and wet, then give the fabric a gentle tug horizontally and vertically (especially in any areas that appear a bit puckered or tight) before letting it soak for at least 20 minutes. I feel like that little tug forces the stitches to shift and relax a little bit before settling down into smooth, even formation.

After soaking, be really gentle with your wet knitting. Handling it too roughly at

this point can result in grossly misshapen garments! If you've been blocking in the sink, let the water drain out *before* picking up your knitting. Press (don't wring!) the excess water out of the knitting before laying it out dry. Do this by wrapping it up in a clean towel and stepping lightly on it.

Lay out your knitting and coax it into the desired measurements, smoothing out any small areas as needed. Many knitters pin the knitting into place on a foam board or towel to help it retain its shape while drying.

When it comes to pins and pinning tools, there are so many options. You can choose simple T-pins or try knit blockers, which are like pin "combs" with multiple pins embedded in each piece. The knit blockers make it really easy to pin straight edges. If you need to block something with extra-long edges, like the Saffron Shawl (page 140) or Kenai Shawl (page 108), try using blocking wires. These long, flexible wires are threaded through the edge of the knitting (when it's still dry), left in place while soaking, and then pinned to a blocking mat to ensure nice straight edges.

Note that it might be necessary to flip thicker fabric (e.g., stranded, double knit, etc.) over several times for it to thoroughly dry.

continued on page 39 »

SWATCH LESSON

IN THIS LESSON you'll practice changing colors, carrying floats, trapping floats, and reading a chart. As you work, you'll refer to the chart below. The gray boxes on each edge of the chart indicate that the stitches should be worked holding both colors together. For additional information on reading charts, see Chart Reading Must-Knows on page 31.

Cast on 19 stitches (or, since each swatch lesson in this book uses 19 sts, continue working on a previously made swatch left over from another chapter). Knit 3 rows to establish a non-curling garter stitch edge.

✤ *Note: For this swatch lesson I worked my swatch flat, back and forth. You should really give stranded purling a try, but if you don't want to purl on the even-numbered rows you can use a circular swatch method (pulling long strands across the back of the work to return to the right-hand side), or you can work a true circular swatch by using a 16" needle to cast on a multiple of 17 stitches (because you will omit the edge stitches) and working several repeats of the chart in the round. I would recommend casting on 68 or 85 stitches.*

Rows 1 and 2: Regardless of how you hold your yarn, these 2 rows will help you practice alternating colors. You won't have to worry about creating perfect floats, since the unused yarn only spans 1 stitch. ❶ shows Row 1 finished.

Rows 3–6: These rows are about switching colors and creating floats that span 3 stitches. Practice creating floats with both the dominant (left) and the non-dominant (right) color on the knit and purl sides of the work. Remember to spread out the stitches on the right needle ❷ before creating your float to ensure a tension that is not too tight. The finished work will look like ❸.

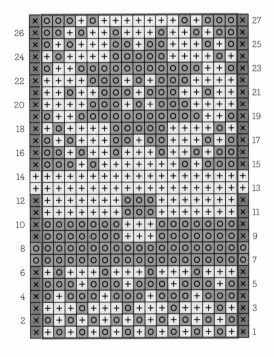

the finished swatch

⊠ hold both colors tog	⊞ light color
⊙ dark color	☐ pattern repeat

Rows 7 and 8: Work stockinette stitch with dark color.

Rows 9–12: Time to trap some super-floats. You'll make 7-stitch floats and trap them somewhere in the middle. You can trap after the third or fourth stitch. It is important to not trap in the same place on each row. If you're working flat for this swatch, the even-numbered rows should be worked on the purl side of your fabric. For detailed steps on trapping floats based on how you are holding yarn, see Trapping Floats, on page 33.

4 shows 3 dark stitches knit and then the needle tip being inserted into the next stitch. The light color is then brought into the way of the next stitch **5**, as if to be used, followed by the dark color **6**. Before the dark stitch is pulled through, the light color is moved out of the way **7** and effectively trapped behind the dark.

If you roll your work slightly forward to look at the back, you will see the light-colored yarn trapped behind the dark stitches **8**.

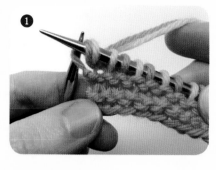

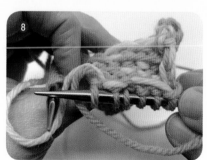

SWATCH LESSON

Here's an example of trapping on the purl side. After you've purled a couple of dark stitches and put the needle tip into the next stitch **9**, wrap the light color over the needle **10** to get it in the way, then wrap the dark color as if to purl **11**, but before pulling it through the stitch, unwrap the light color and pull it out of the way **12**.

13 shows how the light color looks, trapped behind the dark color on the purl side of the work.

Rows 13 and 14: Work stockinette stitch with light color.

Rows 15–27: Follow the chart to work an 8-pointed star motif. Work each row as written, trapping floats when they are longer than 5 stitches. You may have noticed that up to now you've been using the dark as the background and the light as the pattern color. For this section of the motif, the light color becomes the background and the dark color is the pattern, so switch your yarn setup by putting your light color on the right and the dark color on the left.

After completing the chart, bind off all stitches or leave them live to use in a different swatch lesson in the book.

>> *continued from page 35*

Helpful Hints

Gauge too tight? For most people, colorwork knits up at a tighter gauge than normal. So even if you're working with familiar yarn or familiar needles, you really should test out your gauge by knitting a swatch. Don't get too attached to the recommended needle size, because you might find it necessary to use a larger (or smaller) size to get the correct gauge. You could also try forming your stitches around the full diameter of the needle instead of at the needle tip to help them be a little looser.

Stranded purling: Purling and changing colors is no more difficult than knitting and changing colors. Traditionally, stranded colorwork was knit in the round and knitters would use steeks to cut apart the finished garment for finishing work—adding button bands, armholes, etc. (A steek is basically an extra set of stitches worked between two areas of knitted fabric that will eventually be cut apart. The most common locations for using a steek are armholes and neck or collar openings. The cut is made down the middle column of stitches after reinforcements have been made on either side. I include one pattern in this book that uses steeks: the Yukon Jacket, page 132.) The majority of knitters still prefer to work stranded knitting only in the round. Occasionally a design will have you work stranded colorwork on a purl row as well; with a little practice, you'll find it's not as unpleasant as you might think.

You stitched the wrong color: You have two options:

+ Drop the appropriate stitch column down and use the float behind the incorrect stitch to fix the mistake.

+ Or use duplicate stitch to put the correct color in.

Traps showing through? Check to see if floats are too tight. Use the tip of a needle to pull the float back from behind. Also, make sure to block your knitting. It can open up the fibers and help them bloom, making them more able to cover the little bits of floats that pop out from behind. Also, avoid trapping floats in the same spot on subsequent rows.

Dropped stitch? If you're working from a colorwork chart, make sure when you get back to that dropped stitch that you work each stitch directly above it in the correct color so that you maintain the pattern of the chart.

Three colors per row? Try holding the main color in one hand and the other two colors in the other hand. Pay attention to how long each color is not in use so that you can trap it on the edge when needed.

Getting lost within the chart? Use a sticky note to help you keep track of what row you're working from. You can cover up either the rows that you've already worked or the rows that you haven't worked. Try it a couple of different ways until you find a system that works for you and helps you keep track of your row. You can also try using highlighter tape.

Floats too tight? Try turning your work inside out so that the floats occur on the outside of your work. With this method floats are more likely to stay loose.

Forgot to trap a float? Work to the middle of the float on the following row. Put the tip of the needle into the next stitch, slide it under the float from the previous row, then knit the stitch (making sure to only pull the working yarn through and not the float yarn as well).

Combining stranded and intarsia? For tips on combining these two colorwork techniques, see page 60.

5

CHAPTER FIVE

slip stitch & mosaic

EACH KNITTER HAS their own path to follow in regards to what they learn first and how they progress. Maybe you're the type who chose the most complicated project to tackle first. Maybe you've been knitting the same familiar hat pattern over and over again for the past ten years. Whatever your pleasure, slip stitch knitting is something you should try! Do you know how to work a knit stitch? A purl stitch? Can you slide a stitch from one needle to the other? If so, you're ready to give it a shot!

Slip Stitch

The principles of this colorwork technique are fairly basic. Some of the stitches on your left-hand needle will be "worked" and some will be "slipped." These two basic moves yield some really cool results. Yarn position also comes into play with this technique. Typically, when you work a knit stitch, your working yarn is held to the back of your fabric, and when you work a purl stitch it's held to the front. With slip stitch knitting, there is no "typical" rule for yarn position. Sometimes stitches are slipped with the yarn held in back and sometimes they're slipped with the yarn held in front, creating different effects. Slipping stitches leads to the creation of "floats." With this technique, floats can appear on the front or the back and are occasionally incorporated into the stitch pattern itself. The slipped stitches and floats can be manipulated vertically, horizontally, or even diagonally.

One of the most attractive aspects of slip stitch is that you'll never work with more than one color at a time! "How is that possible?" you may ask. Through the magic of slipping stitches, you take what are essentially two-row stripes and manipulate them into graphic motifs and patterns. The resulting fabric can be more dense, firm, and textured than plain stockinette. Slipped stitches that have traveled, in any direction, over their neighboring stitches have a tendency to pull on the fabric (in various directions), affecting row and stitch gauge alike.

What You Need

When choosing yarns for slip stitch colorwork, it's best to consider options that have a bit of elasticity or "give" to them, such as wool, wool blends, or alpaca. Fibers such as cotton, linen, or silk have little to no elasticity and are not as easily manipulated, which leads to uneven, irregular fabrics.

Since you'll only be working with one color at a time, it's not absolutely necessary that the two yarns be identical in fiber or weight. Try experimenting with slip stitch patterns by pairing two yarns together that have different properties.

Chart-Reading Must-Knows

Like most colorwork charts, a right side (RS) row begins on the right and works across to the left. The notations you encounter as you work across will tell you the following information:

+ which stitches to knit

+ which stitches to purl

+ which stitches to slip

+ and whether the slipped stitches should be slipped with the yarn in front of the work (wyf) or with the yarn in the back (wyb).

The box at the top of the page shows some common symbols associated with slip stitch colorwork.

The symbols in the top row all represent the same thing: a stitch that is to be slipped (purlwise) on RS rows with the working yarn held in back. If you encounter the same symbol on a wrong-side (WS) row, you'll slip the stitch with the yarn held in front.

Common symbols for slip stitch

| ⩒ | ⩔ | ⩔ | sl purlwise wyb on RS; sl purlwise wyf on WS |
| ⩒ | ⩔ | ⩔ | sl purlwise wyf on RS; sl purlwise wyb on WS |

The symbols in the bottom row represent a stitch that is to be slipped (purlwise again) on RS rows with the working yarn held in front. The little bar across the "V" or the dot symbolizes the float that results from slipping such a stitch. If you encounter the same symbol on a WS row, it should be slipped with the yarn held to the back.

If you happen to be working a slip stitch pattern in the round, you don't need to worry about changing the directions around for the WS rows. You simply work each stitch as it appears, following the RS row directions.

In most cases, slipped stitches should be slipped purlwise, unless otherwise indicated.

Helpful Hints

Tension: It's very important to handle the yarn loosely when working with slipped stitches. If you tend to be a tighter knitter, try going up a needle size (or two) to avoid too much puckering and pulling of the fabric.

What if you drop a stitch? Dropping a stitch while working any type of slipped stitch pattern can be a little bit overwhelming. Sometimes it's easiest to just rip back to before the dropped stitch and start over from there. If you want to fix it without ripping back, use an identically worked section as your guide to see how that dropped stitch should look row by row. The appearance of the stitch will show you how it has been worked, whether it was slipped (indicated by a tall, elongated stitch) or worked normally.

A WORD TO THE PURLWISE

What does it mean to slip "purlwise" or "as if to purl"? Take the tip of your right-hand needle and insert it into the first stitch on your left-hand needle as if you were going to purl the stitch. Next, simply lift it up a bit and transfer it to the right-hand needle, and, voilá, you've slipped a stitch! If you're asked to work a slipped stitch with the yarn in front, you move the yarn to the front of your work first, slip the stitch, then return the yarn to the back of the work. It's important to always move the yarn back to its original position after working a slipped stitch to avoid creating unwanted yarn overs and extra stitches.

SWATCH LESSON—SLIP STITCH

IN THIS LESSON you'll practice slipping stitches over single and multiple rows and manipulating stitches diagonally. Feel free to continue with live stitches from another chapter or work this lesson by itself.

With the darker color, cast on 19 sts using your preferred method (or, since each swatch lesson in this book uses 19 sts, continue working on a previously made swatch left over from another chapter).

Knit 3 rows, then purl 1 row to create a non-rolling edge ❶. The purl row acts as a foundational row from which you can slip stitches when working the first row of the chart.

Row 1: Begin working from the chart. Attach the lighter color using your preferred method (for more information on attaching a second color, see Chapter Three: Stripes, page 23) and knit the first stitch ❷. According to the chart, the next stitch will be slipped with the yarn held to the back (wyb), as shown in ❸. (Not clear why? See Chart-Reading Must-Knows, page 41.) Continue to work across Row 1, slipping every other stitch.

Row 2: Purl all stitches, including the slipped stitches from Row 1 ❹.

Rows 3 and 4: Use the darker color to work 2 rows.

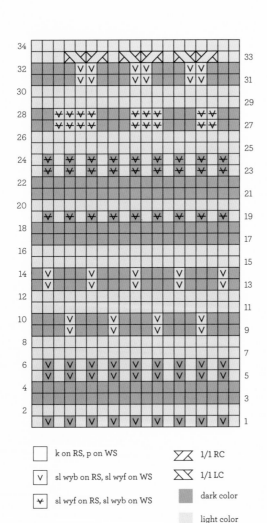

the finished swatch

☐ k on RS, p on WS	⟩⟨ 1/1 RC
V sl wyb on RS, sl wyf on WS	⟩⟨ 1/1 LC
⩒ sl wyf on RS, sl wyb on WS	▨ dark color
	▨ light color

Rows 5 and 6: Now you'll work the same slipped stitches as Row 1, but this time you'll slip them over 2 rows instead of just one. At the beginning of Row 6, purl the first stitch. The next stitch is a slipped stitch from the previous row. Instead of purling it, slip it again. The symbol implies that this stitch should be slipped with the yarn in back, but since you're working a WS row, the stitch gets slipped with the yarn in front or with the yarn to the wrong side of the work. See ❺ and ❻.

❼ shows how it looks after **Row 6.** The dark slipped stitches are as tall as the 2 stacked light stitches.

Rows 7 and 8 set up foundation rows for the slipped stitches in the next pattern motif ❽.

Rows 15 and 16: Use the lighter color to work 2 rows.

Rows 9–14 have you work a brick stitch pattern ❾ and ❿. This is an example of using the slipped stitch in an actual stitch pattern.

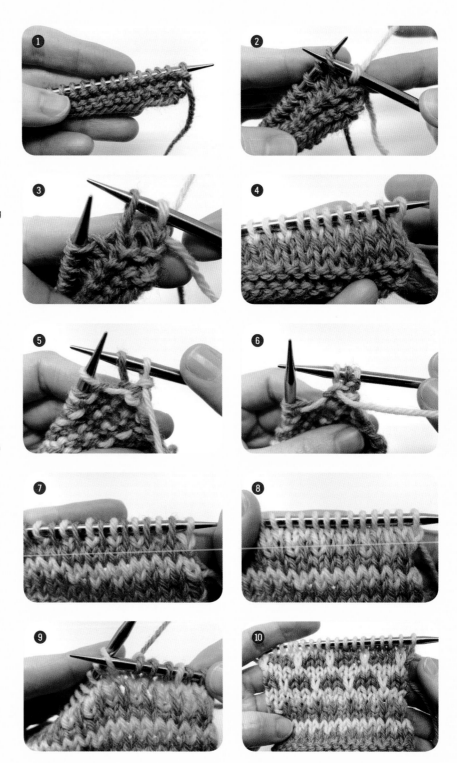

SWATCH LESSON—SLIP STITCH

Rows 17 and 18: Use the darker color to work 2 rows.

Row 19: Knit the first stitch 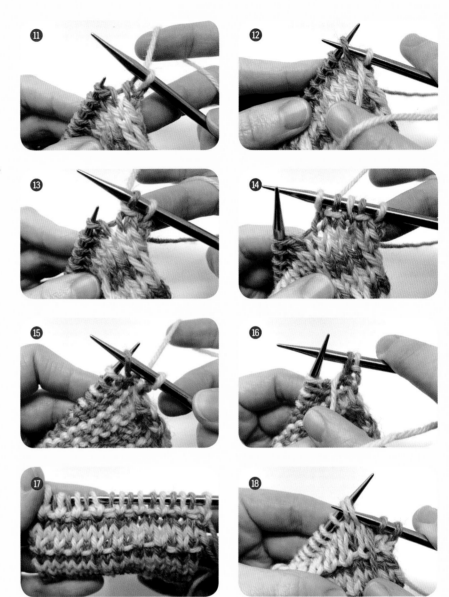, then move the working yarn to the front in preparation for slipping the second stitch.

Slip the next stitch, then move your working yarn to the back. After working a couple of stitches, you'll see the horizontal floats created by slipping with the yarn held in front.

Rows 20–22: Work as shown.

Row 23 gets worked the same as Row 19.

When working **Row 24,** remember that this is a wrong-side row, which means you must make sure your yarn is held in the right place for each stitch. Purl the first stitch, then move the yarn to the back in order to slip the next stitch, as shown in (you're moving your yarn to the "front of the work," but it looks like you're moving it to the back). After you slip the stitch, move the yarn to the front (the "back of the work") in order to purl again.

After **Rows 23 and 24** are worked, your swatch will look like. You'll notice that the floats created by the stitches slipped (wyif) are stacked 2 deep, since you worked 2 rows back-to-back.

Rows 25 and 26: Work 2 additional rows of stockinette in the lighter color.

Rows 27 and 28 help you practice slipping more than 1 stitch at a time. After knitting the first 2 stitches, slip the next 2 stitches (with the yarn held in front), as shown in. You can slip each stitch one at a time, or you can insert the tip of your right-hand needle into both stitches and slip both at the same time (since you'll be slipping them purlwise). After slipping the 2 stitches, move your yarn to the back and then check to make sure the float you just created on the right-hand needle isn't too tight or too loose before knitting the next stitches 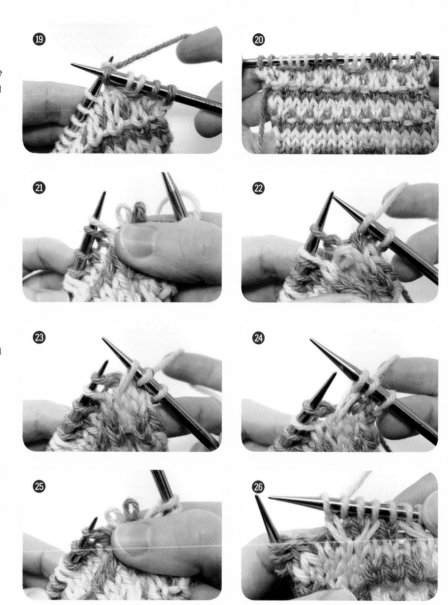.

After completing Row 27, you'll have floats of three different lengths; 2, 3, and 4 stitches ⑳. Row 28 is a WS row, so it is important to keep the yarn in the right position as you work each stitch.

Rows 29 and 30: Work 2 stockinette rows in the light color to set up for the next exercise.

Rows 31–34 have you practice manipulating the slipped stitches to create diagonal lines across the knitted fabric by working 1/1 twists (sometimes referred to as cables or crosses).

Row 33: After knitting the first 2 stitches, it's time to work the first right twist. Here's how to work a 1/1 right twist without having to use a cable needle. Pinch the base of the next 2 stitches with your right hand to hold them in place ㉑. Then use the tip of your left-hand needle to pick up the dark stitch ㉒. Now use your right-hand needle tip to pick up the light-color slipped stitch and put it back on the left needle ㉓. Knit these 2 stitches, which you just twisted ㉔.

Repeat for the next 2 stitches, but with the twist going the other way—a left twist—as shown in ㉕. The set of 2 slipped stitches worked in Rows 31 and 32 are now splayed open diagonally to the left and to the right ㉖. Work the rest of the row in the same way.

After completing Row 34, bind off all stitches.

Mosaic

The term "mosaic knitting" was originally coined by the great Barbara Walker back in the 1960s. She was a pioneer in slip stitch colorwork and really created an amazing foundation for mosaic knitting.

Mosaic knitting is a technique that involves slipped stitches but is governed by stricter rules. For example, slipped stitches in mosaic patterns are always worked with the yarn held to the back of the work, never with the yarn held to the front.

just eliminate one row and simplify the chart. Many knitters find this element of mosaic knitting very enjoyable, because after working a RS row, or odd-numbered round, you do not have to look back to the chart for instruction but can just "read" the last row of knitting and repeat what you just did.

The alternating dark and light squares up the sides of the chart indicate which color to work the row and are referred to

as the "selvedge" stitches. If the selvedge stitch at the edge is dark, then all the dark stitches on that row will be knit and the light stitches will be slipped from the left needle to the right. Work the second row exactly the same as the first, working the dark stitches and slipping the light. Once you return to your starting point, simply drop the dark color and pick up the light. Now it's the light color's turn to knit stitches for two rows while all the

What You Need

Just as for slip stitch knitting, the best yarns for mosaic have a bit of elasticity or "give": wool, wool blends, or alpaca. The yarns need not be identical in fiber or weight.

Chart-Reading Must-Knows

When you read a mosaic chart, the first thing you want to do is look at the numbered rows to figure out how it's charted. Sometimes every row of the pattern will be charted (as in the Saffron Shawl, page 140), and sometimes it'll be a more condensed chart (as in the Swatch Lesson on the facing page). With a condensed chart each row represents 2 rows of knitting! The numbers up the right side of your chart will be listed as 1, 3, 5, 7, etc., and on the direct opposite side as 2, 4, 6, 8, etc. This means that Row 1 is worked from right to left as indicated on the chart and that Row 2 is exactly the same as Row 1, but worked from left to right. Since the stitches in every 2 rows are the same, it's easier to

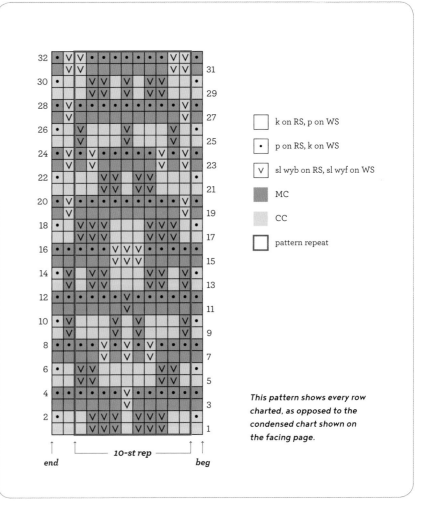

k on RS, p on WS

• p on RS, k on WS

V sl wyb on RS, sl wyf on WS

MC

CC

pattern repeat

This pattern shows every row charted, as opposed to the condensed chart shown on the facing page.

10-st rep

end   *beg*

dark color stitches simply get slipped. You will always knit the first and last stitch of a row (RS and WS) with the working color to maintain a clean edge.

Repeats are indicated by two lines running vertically up the sides of the chart, usually a stitch or two in from the edges. If you're working a mosaic stitch pattern in the round, you will simply eliminate the stitches on the outsides of the repeat lines (including the selvedge stitches) and repeat only the multiple of stitches between the lines.

Helpful Hints

Mosaic knitting in the round? Twist the yarns around each other when switching "working colors" at the beginning of every other round to avoid holes. This means you'll pick up the "new" color from underneath the old one to begin knitting the next round.

Improvising: One of the more challenging things about working within the framework of mosaic rules is that it's harder to improvise or change motifs, because a given color can only be used in a row if it appears as a base color in the row below from which to pull it up.

Borders: Picking up the new color from underneath or behind the old color will create a clean checkerboard edge to your mosaic knitting. If you desire a solid-color border along the edges, the easiest way to achieve this is by picking up the stitches along the edges after your piece is knit and then subsequently binding off all stitches.

SWATCH LESSON—MOSAIC

THERE ARE THREE basic "looks" when it comes to mosaic knitting; this translates to three different ways to work a chart:

The first is to knit each row, creating more of a *garter stitch* effect.

The second is to work in a *stockinette* style and knit the right-side rows while purling the wrong-side rows.

The third is a *combination* of the other two. You can choose to knit every row for all the light-color stitches and work the dark colors in stockinette, or vice versa: work the light stitches all in stockinette and the dark stitches in garter.

This lesson will take you through each variation. You will start by working the chart below in the garter stitch style, then again in stockinette, followed by playing with some combinations of the two styles. The last exercise will have you switching the light and dark colors to work the chart one last time.

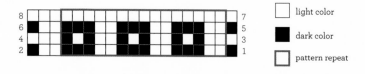

light color

■ dark color

pattern repeat

the finished swatch

SWATCH LESSON—MOSAIC

GARTER STITCH STYLE

With the lighter color, CO 19 sts using preferred method (or, since each swatch lesson in this book uses 19 sts, continue working on a previously made swatch left over from another lesson). Knit 1 row. This first row is not part of the chart but will act as a foundational row from which you can slip stitches when working the first row of the chart.

Row 1: Attach the darker color and begin working from the chart. Knit all of the stitches indicated by black squares (including the first and last stitches, which are the selvedge stitches), and slip the stitches indicated by white squares. Don't be concerned about the light color hanging out at the right side of the work; it will wait patiently for you to return .

Turn the work for **Row 2,** so the WS faces you. Knit the first stitch . Remember, the first and last stitches of the wrong-side rows should always be knit so as to maintain a cleaner edge. Work back across the stitches as they appear, knitting the dark stitches and slipping the already slipped light stitches a second time. Since this is a WS row, make sure to keep the yarn in the right position when slipping the stitches. The yarn should be held to the front of the work when slipping, to create the floats shown in .

Drop the yarn that you just finished working with to the front of your knitting and pick up the new color from behind, as shown in  (in this example it will be the light color that you cast on with). If you begin each right-side row with this pattern, you will create a neat, striped edging up the side of your work.

Knit the first stitch with the light color .

pro tip / *After knitting the first stitch, give a little tug to the dark yarn that you just finished with to help tighten up the first stitch.*

Work **Row 3** of the chart by knitting all the squares that are light and slipping all the ones that are dark. Turn the work and work **Row 4** by knitting all the light stitches and slipping all the dark ones (with the yarn in front or to the WS of the fabric).

Rows 5 and 6 are worked just the same as Rows 1 and 2. Drop the light yarn that you just finished with to the front of the work and pick up the dark yarn from the back to begin knitting .

Rows 7 and 8 of this chart are simple garter stitch rows worked with the light color, no slipped stitches . These rows create space before the next repeat of the chart during this mosaic stitch lesson.

STOCKINETTE STYLE

Work 2 rows in stockinette stitch using the lighter color.

Now work **Rows 1–8** of the chart again, but this time knit all stitches on the right side of the work and purl all stitches on the wrong side.

✛ Note: *Even though you'll be purling WS rows, you'll still knit the first and last stitches of the row to help maintain a neat edge to your work.*

After completing these rows you'll be able to compare these two mosaic styles. Notice how the chart worked in garter stitch has a much more compact look than the same chart worked in stockinette, which appears more elongated and stretched .

COMBINATION STYLE

Work 2 rows of garter stitch (knit RS and WS) using the lighter color.

For this third time through the chart you'll mix up the two methods you just practiced. You'll work Rows 1–8 again, this time working the light-color stitches in the garter stitch method and the dark-color stitches in the stockinette method.

Rows 1 and 2 are worked with the dark color first, knitting all the dark squares on Row 1 and purling those same stitches when working back across Row 2 .

On **Rows 3 and 4,** knit all the light squares, remembering to move the yarn to the correct position (in front) when slipping stitches on Row 4. **Rows 5–8**

will be worked the same as Rows 1–4, working the light color in garter stitch and the dark in stockinette. The resulting combination looks like .

Next, try working **Rows 1–8** with the reverse combination of what you just did. Switch to working the light color in stockinette and the dark color in garter stitch .

REVERSED COLORS

This last variation is more of a mind exercise than anything else. So far, in reference to the chart, you have worked light-color squares with a light-color yarn. What if instead you wanted your background color to be dark? For this to work, you have to tell your mind that the light-color squares are to be knit with your darker yarn and vice versa. With a little practice you'll see the chart

not in terms of "light and dark" but as "background and foreground," and you'll be more comfortable switching up light and dark yarns.

Work 2 rows of garter stitch with your dark yarn. Work **Rows 1–8** with the colors reversed, and feel free to choose whichever method you prefer: garter, stockinette, or combined .

6

intarsia

THE WORD INTARSIA HAS Italian roots tied to the art form of marquetry—inlays with wood. In relation to knitting, you will create inlays of color within your fabric, using a separate ball of yarn, or yarn supply, for each color section.

For many, intarsia is synonymous with tangles and frustration. However, with a little bravery and attention to detail, this technique can be a painless method of incorporating multiple colors into your knitting projects. So what's the secret? As with most things, the road to success is paved with a little preparation and groundwork, and it doesn't hurt to know some tricks and have the right tools. Take a deep breath, focus, and learn this technique one step at a time. After all, intarsia is not much different from stockinette—knit on one side, purl on the other. The new challenge with this technique is managing the different colors and yarn supplies.

Intarsia allows you to incorporate large areas of multiple colors into your knitting without having to worry about carrying yarns and managing floats. You can create pictorial motifs as well as simple shapes, polka-dots, or color blocking. The resulting fabric has both the drape of stockinette and the appeal of colorwork. It may not be the quickest form of colorwork, but it's not difficult.

What You Need

Choosing yarn: Most types of yarn will work well for this technique. Here are a few helpful pointers:

Use a yarn with a tighter spin, such as a worsted spun, to ensure clearly defined color changes.

Finer-gauge yarns (i.e., fingering, DK, or sport) will allow you to work in more detail and create smoother lines of interlocking colors than chunky yarns.

Yarn supplies: One of the identifiers of intarsia knitting is the numerous bobbins, or yarn supplies, hanging off the back of your work. There are several different types of bobbins available (see right) and you may like some better than others. Take time to prepare the yarn that you'll need before starting your project. Your chart will help you identify how many different yarn supplies to prepare. (See Chart-Reading Must-Knows on page 53 for more information.)

Bobbins come in many styles and sizes. The two at left are flat plastic. The convex side of the translucent donut-shaped bobbins at right flips up for easy winding.

Preparing Yarn Supplies

You'll need a separate supply of yarn for every section of color on your chart. For very large areas of color you might use the full skein (wound into either a ball or a cake), but for smaller areas you have different options, and they don't all involve plastic bobbins.

WINDING BOBBINS

These can be commercially made plastic contraptions or small rectangles you cut from cardboard. For the donut-shaped bobbins, simply flip up the edge of the convex side, wind a small amount of yarn around the center, then push the bobbin closed once more.

Depending on the type of flat plastic bobbin you use, how you wind the yarn may differ slightly, but the general technique remains the same: Hold one end of the yarn firmly in place against the flat side of the bobbin ❶. Wind the desired length

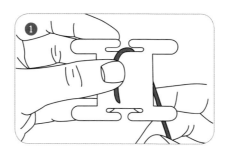

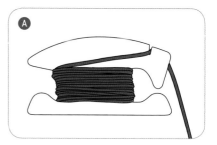

of yarn around the width of the bobbin, making sure to cover and secure the yarn end ❷, then secure the tail into the designated guide or slot ❸. Securing the yarn may differ slightly depending on the bobbin, as shown in Ⓐ and Ⓑ.

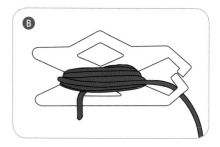

MAKING BUTTERFLIES

Use this method to create small, light-weight yarn supplies without using a plastic bobbin.

1 Place the yarn across the palm of your hand and secure the end attached to the skein between your thumb and hand **1**.

2 Wrap the yarn in a figure-eight pattern between your pinky and thumb **2** until you have the amount you desire. Measure out an additional 6–8" (15–20.5 cm) tail, then cut the yarn.

3 Wrap the 6–8" (15–20.5 cm) tail around the middle of the butterfly several times and then tuck the end underneath one of the wraps **3**. When you use the butterfly later, don't pull from this tucked-in end; instead, pull from the other end **4**.

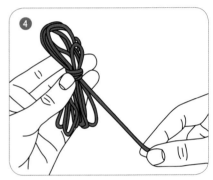
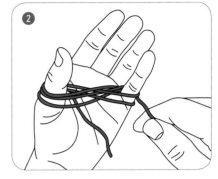
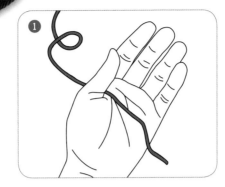

CUT-YARN METHOD

Another way to manage yarn supplies is to simply let them hang without any winding at all. It may sound counterintuitive for keeping the ends free of tangles, but think how easy it is to simply pull one yarn strand out of a small tangle with nothing encumbering it! With this method it's advisable to use yarn lengths no longer than about 3–5 feet (0.9–1.5 m).

Attaching a New Yarn Supply

See page 23 for ways to attach a new color mid-row.

HOW MUCH YARN SHOULD YOU WIND?

Count the number of stitches in your color area. Wrap the yarn around your needle the same amount of times—because one wrap of yarn around your needle gives you an approximation of one stitch. Then unwrap the yarn and add 8–10" (20.5–25.5 cm) on either end to account for margin of error as well as for finishing. Wind this amount into a butterfly or a bobbin.

If you choose to simply estimate the amount of yarn (instead of calculate), just remember that it doesn't need to be exact. If you're working with natural fibers, you can always splice in more yarn or attach a new yarn supply. One word of caution, though: The more yarn you wind up, the heavier the yarn supply will be, causing possible distortions in the fabric and/or problems with your tension.

Chart-Reading Must-Knows

Much like in stranded knitting, each row of an intarsia chart represents a row of knitting and shows which stitches to work in each color. In order to determine how many separate yarn supplies to prepare, you should identify the row of the chart that shows the greatest number of color changes.

You'll need a yarn supply for each occurrence of any given color. So, if a given row shows four different areas of main color

divided up by other colors, you will need four separate balls of the main color and a ball for each of the other colors that appear in the row.

The illustration below shows an intarsia chart that has been marked up to give you an idea of how you would go about planning yarn supplies and strategies for knitting. The column on the left indicates how many yarn supplies you need for any given row.

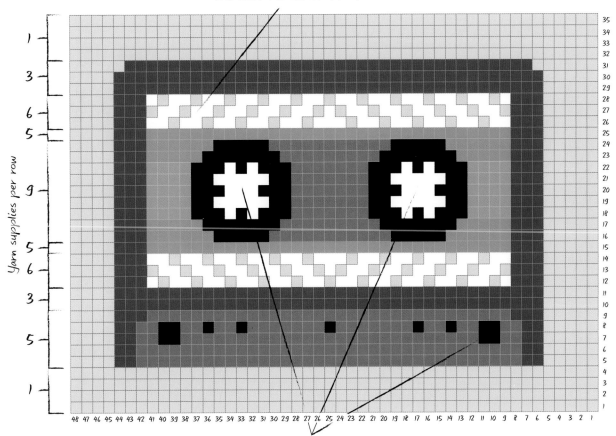

This section is stranded work.

Yarn supplies per row

These sections are made in duplicate stitch: the small details, and also the white centers of these black circles.

Working Intarsia in the Round

Knitting intarsia in the round is an illusion. It's impossible to work intarsia in the round, because yarn supplies are always left hanging at the far end, or left side, of the section just worked. However, the following methods provide clever workarounds that allow you to basically knit flat back and forth but keep the beginnings and ends of the rows connected, creating the illusion of knitting in the round.

METHOD 1: YARN OVERS

Add a yarn over (yo) at the beginning of each row. It will fall between the first and last stitch of the row. When you come to the last stitch of the row, work it together with the yo, either as an ssk on RS rows or as a p2tog on WS rows. Then turn your work and make another yo right away before proceeding to work the next row.

METHOD 2: SLIPPED STITCHES

This method creates a visible "seam" and only works if the two colors you're joining are the same. Add an additional stitch at the end of the round by casting on one more stitch than required. At the beginning of each row, slip the extra stitch and then work to the end (including the slipped stitch). Turn your work, slip the extra stitch, and work to the end. Continue in this pattern.

Wrapped Stitches

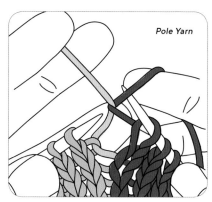

Pole Yarn

METHOD 3: WRAPPED STITCHES

Work to the end of your first row, slip the first stitch of the next round, and wrap the yarn around it before slipping it back to the left-hand needle, as if working a wrap-and-turn on a short-row (see the illustration above, left). Turn your knitting and work the next row. When you get to the wrapped stitch, work the wrap together with the stitch (use a ssk on the knit side and a p2tog on the purl side) and then slip and wrap the next stitch. Turn the work again and continue working in this manner. This method tends to produce a tighter join than the others.

METHOD 4: POLE YARN

This method uses a separate piece of yarn as a "pole." Wrap your working yarn around this pole at the end of each row before turning your work and proceeding with the next row (see the yellow yarn in the illustration above, right). Remember to tie the pole yarn in at the beginning and end, or else one good pull could be your downfall.

continued on page 59 »

SWATCH LESSON

IN THIS LESSON you'll practice attaching a new yarn, working with two, three, and four yarn supplies, and vertical and horizontal color changes. Before starting the lesson, prepare four yarn supplies; two of the light color and two of the dark color. As you work, refer to the chart below.

Using the darker yarn, CO 19 stitches (or, since each swatch lesson in this book uses 19 sts, continue working on a previously made swatch left over from another chapter).Work 3 rows of knitting if this is a new swatch, to prevent curling.

Row 1: Knit 9 stitches, join new color using one of the methods listed on page 23. For intarsia especially, I recommend using Method 1.

Knit 10 sts with new color. Turn the work and purl back on Row 2 to the point of the color change ❶. To avoid a hole when changing from one color to another you need to perform a "twist or interlock" with the yarns. To do this, drop the yarn that you just finished working with (the "old color") over the top, or to the left, of the "new color" ❷.

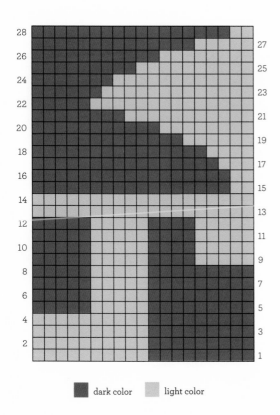

	dark color		light color

the finished swatch

SWATCH LESSON

Pick up the new color from underneath, or to the right of, the old color ; it's now ready to use . Working the old and new colors in this manner "twists" them around each other and creates the interlock that prevents holes! This will work no matter where the color change happens or whether you are on a knit or purl row.

Row 3: Work to the point of the color change . 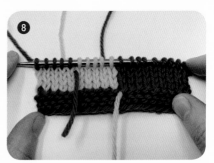 shows how the twist looks on the back when working a RS row. The old color gets moved over the top of the new one, before working with the new one.

Row 4: Work according to the chart. You now have 4 rows complete 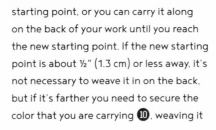.

Row 5: Following the chart, knit 9 stitches of dark color, 5 stitches of light color, and then attach the second dark yarn supply and knit the last 5 stitches. You're now working with three yarn supplies in 1 row . For suggestions on managing multiple yarn supplies, see the section called Tangles?, on page 61.

Rows 6–8: Follow the chart, working vertical color changes as established with three yarn supplies.

Row 9: On this row, you introduce a fourth yarn supply at the beginning of the row 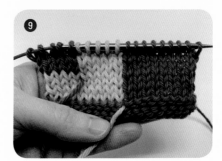.

You'll notice the darker yarn supply was left hanging at the right side of the work upon completion of the last row. Since you need to move it 5 stitches to the left now, you have two options. You can either cut the dark yarn and reattach it at its new starting point, or you can carry it along on the back of your work until you reach the new starting point. If the new starting point is about ½" (1.3 cm) or less away, it's not necessary to weave it in on the back, but if it's farther you need to secure the color that you are carrying 🔟, weaving it

in along the WS of the work . (See page 33 in the chapter on stranded knitting for more information on securing floats on the WS of your work.)

Rows 10–12: Work vertical color changes where indicated, managing four yarn supplies. Before beginning each row, make sure that the needle has gone under all the yarn supplies  before being inserted into the first stitch.  shows the completed rows.

For the next part of the lesson you'll practice horizontal color changes, meaning they won't occur stacked on top of each other but will instead be 1, 2, or 3 stitches apart. These types of color changes are found in intarsia designs that have curved lines.

Rows 13 and 14: Work 2 rows of stockinette stitch with the lighter color. At this point you can cut off the other three yarn supplies and leave tails 2–3" (5–7.5 cm) long hanging on the WS of the work . You can weave these in later or weave them in as you knit across, as shown in .

Rows 15 and 16: Attach the darker yarn supply where indicated .

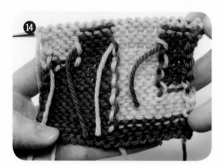

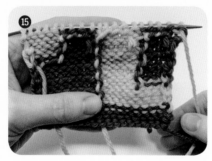

SWATCH LESSON

Row 17: This is the first time the color change doesn't happen vertically. Knit 3 stitches with the light color 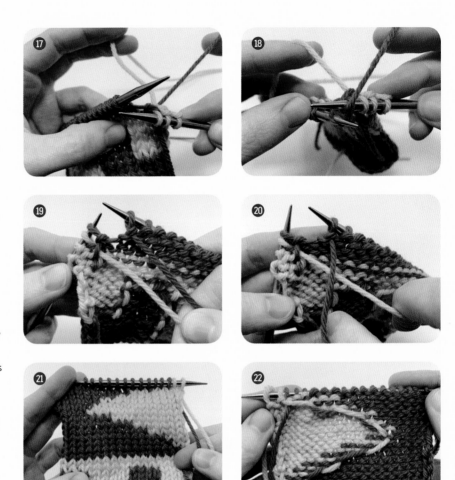 and then, as established before, drop the old (light green) color to the left of the new (dark) color, pick up the new color from the right, and begin to knit with it ⑱.

Row 18: On the WS row you will work the light color 1 stitch earlier than the previous row. This change is tricky because of the position of each yarn supply at the time of the color change. Nonetheless, drop the old color off on the left side of the new color, crossing it over the top of the yarn supply ⑲ and ⑳, and pick up the new color from underneath the old.

Rows 19–28 give you a chance to practice more horizontal color changes occurring 1, 2, and 3 stitches apart. As your changes get farther apart, take care to not pull your new yarn too tightly or leave it hanging too loose when switching colors. Practice leaving the perfect amount that will allow the work to lie flat by making sure the stitches are spread out evenly and the fabric is lying flat before working stitches of new color. Work as indicated on the chart. ㉑ shows how the front of your work looks after completing Row 28, and ㉒ shows the back.

Bind off all stitches, or leave them live to practice a different colorwork technique from another chapter.

continued from page 54 »

Duplicate Stitch

Technically speaking, duplicate stitch is a form of embroidery, worked onto knitted fabric, that mimics the look of the knit stitch. It can be incredibly handy when filling in small areas of color or tiny details consisting of only a stitch or two. If a small detail on your chart is worked in the same color as a larger area nearby, consider leaving a considerable tail (up to 24" [61 cm]) at the end of the larger section to be used for executing the duplicate stitch area. Get a tapestry needle and work it as follows.

✦ **Note:** *It's easiest to work duplicate stitch from bottom to top and from the right to the left, so plan your stitches accordingly.*

1 Cut a piece of yarn about 2 feet (61 cm) long and thread the tapestry needle. With your needle on the WS of the fabric, bring the tip through the middle of the stitch below the one you want to cover ❶.

2 Follow the right leg of the "V" (the shape of your stitch) up and insert the needle behind the two legs of the V in the stitch directly above ❷. Pull the yarn through, but not too tightly; you're trying to perfectly match the tension of the stitch that you're covering up.

3 Now insert the needle back into the middle of the stitch below, right where you initially started ❸, and pull through to the WS.

❹ shows the completed stitch. Work each stitch exactly the same way, whether stacked vertically, horizontally, or in any other pattern.

❺ and ❻ show the front and back sides of the same piece with duplicate stitching.

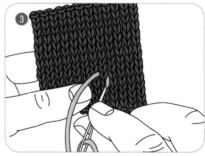

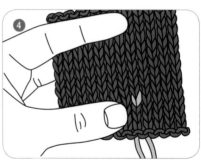

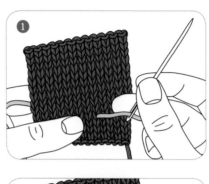

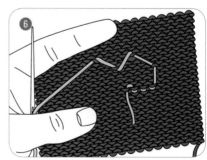

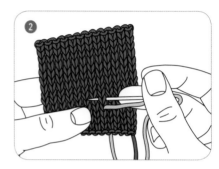

Combining Intarsia and Stranded Knitting

Combining these two colorwork techniques can be tricky, because stranded fabric is thicker and not quite as elastic as intarsia fabric. You want to make sure that the resulting combination doesn't pucker or bunch up. If you can get the balance right, it turns out looking super cool!

The key to making this combination work is to treat the two strands of yarn that you use in the stranded section as just one yarn when it comes time to make a color change. The top illustration at right shows a chart where the left side is worked in a solid color and the right side is a stranded pattern.

Here's an example of how this works. Work to the color change ❶, drop the two strands of yarn together over to the left, as if they were one strand ❷, and pick up the single strand of the next color section from underneath ❸. If you roll the work forward you can see the two yarns from the stranded section intertwined with the solid color from the other section ❹.

Sometimes you'll have a color in the stranded section that also appears outside of it, such as a white and blue stranded motif with solid white on either side. Instead of carrying that white color through the stranded section, you should use three different white supplies, one in the stranded section and then one for each side. Doing it this way will significantly reduce the amount of pulling and puckering that would happen if you carried the same white yarn across all the sections.

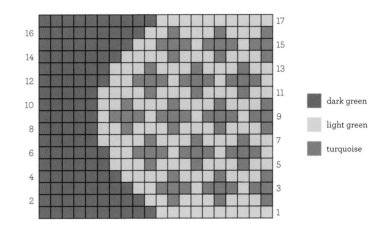

	dark green
	light green
	turquoise

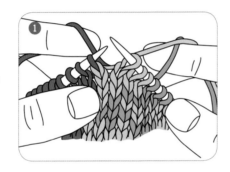

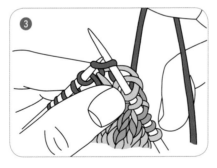

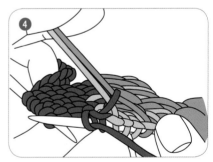

Helpful Hints

Textured stitch patterns: Although typically worked in stockinette, intarsia can also incorporate textured stitch patterns (e.g., moss stitch or rib stitch) to add interest to the fabric or picture. If you want to use a textured stitch pattern, it's important that you always work the first row of any new color in stockinette (knit all stitches on the RS, purl on the WS). Failing to do so will result in visible purl bumps of the wrong color in the textured section.

Using DPNs: When using double-pointed needles to knit in the round, don't place the intersections of colors between two needles. If the join falls somewhere in the middle of the stitches on any given needle, your stitches will be more uniform and less likely to look sloppy and oversized.

Tangles? Managing yarn is one of the biggest challenges with intarsia knitting. There is no magical "one way" for everyone, because a lot of it has to do with your personality. If you'd rather avoid tangles altogether, try laying your yarn supplies out in the order they will be worked, and twisting the yarn supplies in the appropriate direction as you come to each color change. If you don't mind a little work, you can simply stop every couple of rows and untangle any mess that has occurred. If all else fails and you feel ready to tear your hair out, consider just cutting the offending yarn out of the mess and splicing a new yarn supply onto it!

Holes? For directions on interlocking your yarns, see the last paragraph on page 55. If you notice a hole in your knitting after you've finished, the first thing you should do is look for a nearby tail on the back side of the work and see if it can be brought close enough to the hole to close it up. If there is not a tail nearby, you can still fix it with an entirely new piece of yarn and a darning needle, weaving in the ends when done.

Uneven stitches? This is common when working with vertical color changes. The best way to avoid this pitfall is by working to the point of the color change and creating your "interlock" or twist of the yarns before inserting your needle tip into the next stitch. Inserting the needle tip distorts the shape of the stitch on the row below. It's worth a bit of extra practice to develop even tension and make sure you are not pulling too tightly on the new yarn when switching colors (creating tightened and collapsed stitches) or letting the new yarn hang too loosely (creating oversized, relaxed stitches) when you pick it up to work with it. If you didn't notice the unevenness before you finished, you can still go back and use a blunt needle or knitting needle to gently reshape each stitch until you have uniformity. This method is particularly effective when done while wet blocking your knitting, allowing the newly reformed stitches to dry in their even shapes.

Weaving in tails: Tails left on the RS of the work need to be brought to the back with either a crochet hook or a tapestry needle. Before weaving, give the end a slight tug to tighten up any loose stitches and to see if it is properly interlocked with the stitches next to it. Move the end around a bit while looking at the right side of the work; this will give you the best idea of which direction to weave it in. Aim for weaving your ends into the "links" on the WS that result from interlocking your colors. This way they won't be visible from the front.

7

CHAPTER SEVEN

double knitting

DOUBLE KNITTING IS a lot like the shy neighbor kid who was always around but never spoke much. It's a colorwork technique that hasn't received the same level of attention that other techniques have. When you give it a chance, you might be surprised at how fun and useful it can be. Think of double-layered hats and mittens for cold climates or double-knit heels on your favorite socks that get worn constantly. With double knitting you're essentially creating two layers of fabric at the same time, usually with the knit sides facing outward and the purl sides facing each other. Double knitting can be worked in a single color, but in this book you'll explore the two-color basics.

How does it work? Every stitch belongs to a pair of stitches called a Double Stitch Pair (DSP). Each DSP is made up of a knit stitch of one color and a purl stitch of the other color. The knit stitch belongs to the top layer of fabric being created while the purl stitch belongs to the bottom layer. Since you're alternating knit and purl stitches, this technique can feel a lot like k1, p1 ribbing, but working every other stitch with a different color creates its own unique fabric. As you work across the needle, alternating knit and purl stitches, you move your yarns back and forth as a pair. They always move as a pair, no matter which color is working the next stitch.

As with most other colorwork techniques in this book, the way you hold your yarn is highly individual and completely up to you. Do what feels comfortable. An important thing to remember is that you should try to always maintain the same arrangement of colors (e.g., main color to the right, contrast color to the left, etc.). For more information on ways to hold yarn, see page 31.

One last note: Double knitting (or DK, as we'll refer to it) provides an amazing canvas for creativity when it comes to charting. With this technique you never have to worry about floats of any size, since both colors are used in every DSP. This means the sky is the limit for design ideas! So, let's get started.

What You Need

I recommend a medium-weight yarn, anywhere from a sport or DK up to possibly an aran weight. It will be trickier to get good results from really fine or really chunky yarns (and, yes, it's slightly confusing that the abbreviation for double knitting is DK and there's also a yarn weight called DK!).

You may also want to choose to use an aid for separating colors, depending on how you hold your yarn. For more information on managing colors, see the section on gadgets, on page 31.

Casting On

There are more than a few methods for casting on and binding off with this technique. Some are quick; some aren't. Below, you'll find a few of my favorite methods for casting on and binding off.

2-strand long tail cast-on: This method is worked by holding two strands of the same color together (main color) and casting on the desired number of DSPs. Since you're holding two strands together, each "stitch" you cast on is actually the equivalent of one DSP. (For example, if you need 20 stitches for your project, 20 stitches = 10 DSPs, so you would cast on 10.) The second color is introduced on the first row by knitting the first stitch of the pair with the cast-on color and then purling the second stitch with the other color. This is a quick cast-on option that is fairly neat and clean  and .

1 *2-strand long tail cast-on, right side*

2 *2-strand long tail cast-on, wrong side*

3 *Italian two-color cast-on*

Italian two-color cast-on 3: For instructions on how to work this cast-on method, see the Glossary (page 153). This cast-on gives you a clean, stretchy beginning to each side with no opposite colors showing through. However, the edge it produces is slightly hollow and puffy and doesn't lie as flat as the others.

Binding Off

With double knitting, a standard bind-off will essentially double the width of your fabric and stretch out the bound-off edge. If you want to use the standard bind-off, you'll need to either work the stitches of each DSP together or else eliminate one stitch of the pair before binding off.

Condensed bind-off: This easy-to-work bind-off results in a firm, solid edge without creating extra width (4 and 5). Its main downside is that it's not very stretchy, which could be a desirable effect, depending on your project. With the main color, k1, p1, k1, then pass the first stitch over the other two. Continue to work one stitch at a time and pass the first stitch over the other two. When you have two stitches left, pass the first stitch over the second, then close up the last stitch.

Grafted edge 6: To get a clean, seamless finish you can divide the layers and then graft them together using Kitchener stitch (see Glossary). This bind-off is the perfect match to the Italian Two-Color Cast-On, and just like its counterpart, it tends to feel a little puffy and not lie as flat as other bind-offs.

4 *Condensed bind-off, right side*

5 *Condensed bind-off, wrong side*

6 *Grafted edge*

SINGLE TO DOUBLE (AND BACK!)

To transition from single-layer knitting to double knitting, the first thing you need to do is establish DSPs. Essentially, each single stitch needs to be doubled. An easy way to do this is knitting into the front and back of each stitch, creating a DSP from every stitch. With this method you'll introduce the second color on the following row.

If you want to introduce the second color on the setup row, then you need to knit into the front of the stitch with the first color and then purl into the back of the stitch with the other color. With this method, make sure you move both colors back and forth as you work the setup row, just like you would in established double knitting.

After you're done double knitting, you can revert back to single-layer knitting by working each pair together with an ssk (the right-leaning decrease is important, because it'll help keep the correct stitch on top).

The Perfect Edge

It's very important to give your side edges (also called selvedges) some attention in double knitting. There are several ways to ensure that the two layers are attached on the right and left sides. Here are two of my favorites:

2-color slip stitch selvedge 7: At the beginning of the row, slip the first DSP purlwise as one unit. Work to the last DSP (2 sts) and k2tog (using both colors). Repeat on each row. This method is quick and easy, but it does leave you with a two-color edge that isn't as clean as the next option.

Perfect slip stitch selvedge 8:

✦ *Note: Maintain color position as you work this selvedge by holding the main color to the right and the contrast color to the left.*

1 RS row: Work to the last DSP (2 sts). With both colors in back, slip the knit stitch (purlwise), cross the main color yarn over the top of the contrast color, and then move only the contrast color to the front before slipping the last st (also purlwise). Leave the contrast color in the front and the main color in the back.

2 WS row: Work to the last DSP. With both colors in back, slip the knit stitch purlwise, then move only the main color to the front (without the crossover) before slipping the last stitch purlwise. Leave the main color in the front and the contrast color in the back.

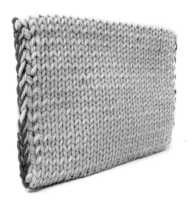

7 *2-color slip stitch selvedge*

8 *Perfect slip stitch selvedge*

Chart-Reading Must-Knows

As mentioned in the introduction, this technique opens up endless possibilities for charting and design. Here's what you'll need to know to navigate a DK chart.

In most other colorwork techniques, each box on the chart represents one stitch in the knitting. With DK, both sides of the knitting are represented in the same chart, meaning that each box represents a DSP (a knit stitch followed by a purl stitch). The color of the box indicates only the knit stitch color (on the RS of the work). It's up to you to complete the pair by making a purl stitch with the color *not* indicated.

For example, in the chart shown at right, the lighter-colored squares represent Main Color DSPs (knit stitch is worked with the main color and purl stitch with the contrast color). The darker squares represent Contrast Color DSPs (knit stitch worked with the contrast color and purl stitch with the main color).

The two sides of double-knit fabric are negative/mirror images of each other. Every time you make a color change in DK,

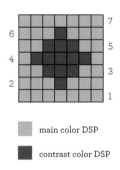

main color DSP

contrast color DSP

the two layers of fabric become locked together. A DK chart shows you what's happening on the Right Side (RS) of the fabric *only*. If you're working flat (that is, knitting back and forth), you'll have to adjust your brain to reverse the pattern for WS rows. When working in the round you don't need to worry about reversing the chart in your head, since the same side is always facing you. Just a little FYI: It's possible to have different images on each side of double knitting, but that's beyond the scope of this chapter, and a whole other book could be written about it!

continued on page 69 »

SWATCH LESSON

IN THIS LESSON you'll practice changing colors, reading a chart, and increases and decreases. Follow along with the chart below.

If you're continuing with live stitches from another swatch lesson, see the sidebar called Single to Double (and Back!), on page 64. If you're working this lesson as a stand-alone swatch, choose one of the cast-on options listed on page 63.

Cast on 19 DSPs for a total of 38 sts. **1** shows the two-strand long tail cast-on, and **2** shows how the stitches look on the needle.

Row 1: Knit into the first strand of the first DSP with the main color **3**, then attach the contrast color and pull both colors to the front before purling the second strand stitch **4**. Move both yarns to the back and repeat the knit and purl stitches across the row. Remember to move both yarns as one, always together, forward and back between each stitch! **5** shows Row 1 completed.

Row 2 is a WS row, with the contrast-color knit stitches facing you instead of the main color. For each DSP you will work the knit stitches in the contrast color followed by the purl stitches in the main color.

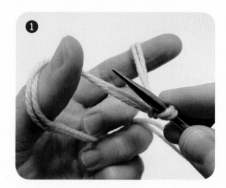

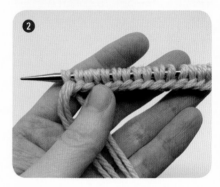

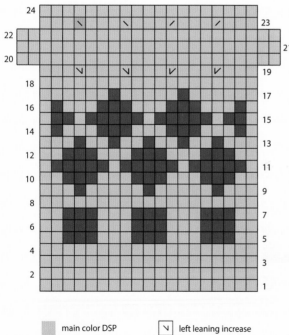

the finished swatch

	main color DSP		$\diagdown$	left leaning increase
	contrast color DSP		$\diagup$	k2tog on MC side, ssp on CC side
$\vee$	right leaning increase		$\diagdown$	ssk on MC side, p2tog on CC side

Remember to move the yarns together back and forth between each stitch. 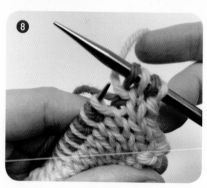 shows the row in progress.

Rows 3 and 4 are worked the same as Rows 1 and 2—however, if you keep going without any consideration for the edges, you'll end up with two separate, unconnected layers. So starting with Row 3, choose your preferred edging method (see page 65) and work accordingly. This swatch lesson shows the perfect slip stitch selvedge method 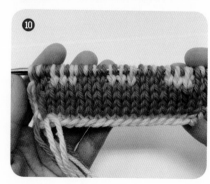.

Rows 5–8 introduce you to simple colorwork changes. Small squares are among the easiest shapes to learn within DK colorwork, because the edges of the shape are just stacked stitches of the same color. The first stitch will be the selvedge edge stitch, and then there is one more Main Color DSP . The third DSP is a Contrast Color DSP and the first color-change "opportunity." The contrast color is used for the knit stitch, and the main color is used for the purl stitch. Note how the contrast-color stitches in  are sitting next to each other. That's not a problem. It's simply an indication of a color change. For more information on reading DK charts, see Chart-Reading Must-Knows (page 65).

Row 6 (WS) is worked with the contrast-color side facing you 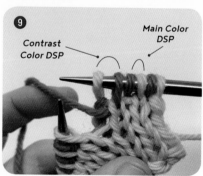. The chart shows your knitting from the main-color side, so you'll have to reverse the colors in your mind as you work.

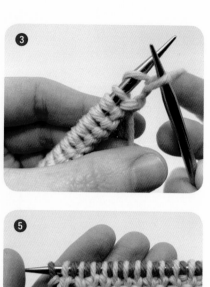

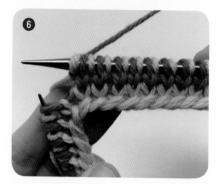

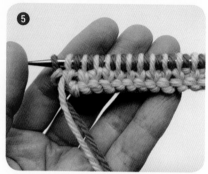

Contrast Color DSP

Main Color DSP

SWATCH LESSON

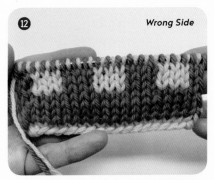 and 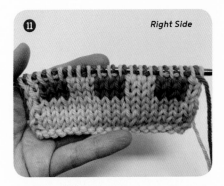 show the completed Rows 5–8, front and back.

Right Side

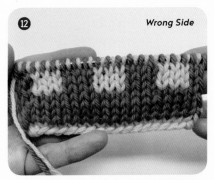

Wrong Side

Rows 9–18: The next rows of pattern are a bit more complex than the squares. You'll find it helpful to just focus on the color of the knit stitch in the DSP and then always follow it up with whatever the "other" color would be. 🔴 and 🔴 show these rows completed.

Row 19: Now that you've challenged yourself with a little chart reading, practice some shaping moves to finish things off. This row is all about increases, two that lean to the left and two that lean to the right. Work 3 DSPs and stop at the fourth. To work the lifted increase 🔴, follow the instructions in the box called Shaping Tips, on page 71.

Right Side

Wrong Side

🔴 shows the RH needle tip position in picking up the right leg of the stitch on the main side, 🔴 shows the leg of the stitch on the back side, and 🔴 shows how the new DSP looks before proceeding with the next 2 slipped stitches.

Row 23: Now it's time to try out some decrease moves! 🔴 shows the two DSPs that will be involved in the decrease. Before the decrease can be executed, rearrange the stitches so that the colors lie next to each other 🔴. After rearranging, work the decrease on the main side and then again on the contrast side 🔴.

Each decrease on this row is worked in the same fashion: Rearrange the correct DSPs, then work decreases on each side separately.

Increase into this stitch.

After completing the last row of the chart, choose your desired method to bind off all stitches (see page 64). If you plan to continue with another swatch lesson, you can work the next row by combining each DSP using ssk. This will take your stitch count back down to 19.

18 This DSP is the result of the increase.

19 These are the 2 DSPs to be combined.

20

21

continued from page 65 »

Helpful Hints

Weaving in ends: Double knitting is hollow, so you can weave your ends in between the layers! Pass ends through color changes because they tend to be a bit tighter.

Large/loose stitches at the edges: Try to work those stitches closer to the tip of the needle, where the diameter is smaller. Avoid putting two full needles into any one stitch.

Open edges: See The Perfect Edge (page 65).

Bars across stitches: Whether on the front or back, this is usually the result of not moving both yarns together when bringing them forward or back. This can be fixed by working to the offending column, dropping the stitch down on the appropriate side of the work, and getting rid of the bar by pulling the trapped stitch under the bar and putting it on the front of the work again, and reworking the stitch back up to the needle.

Missed color change: Work, or unknit, to the column in which the mistake was made. Drop the stitches down on each side to the spot where the mistake occurred. Use a crochet hook to pull the correct color to the correct side and re-create the column according to the chart. It's helpful to be working with a grippy yarn in these situations!

What's happening to the gauge? DK stitches tend to be a little wider than their stockinette counterparts. This is because the stitches don't sit side by side on the needle—they alternate needle space with stitches from the other side of the fabric. Because of this fact, there's just a little extra yarn between stitches, and it contributes to the slightly wider shape. Try sizing down a needle size or two!

Dropped stitch? To put it plainly, this problem doesn't have an easy solution. Dropping a solitary stitch can throw off your pattern of DSPs, and the easiest fix is—unfortunately—ripping back to the point right before the mistake occurred.

Reading a DK pattern: Instead of references to stitches, the pattern will reference DSPs (for example, "work 3 DSPs" or "Dec 1 DSP").

shaping tips

*Let me touch briefly on the topic of shaping with this colorwork technique. This is by no means a full tutorial but rather a few words about the basic principles involved. Whether you're adding a stitch or taking one away, remember that you're working with two layers of fabric. So, whatever you do to one side, you **must** also do to the other side. Not only that, but since the two sides of DK are mirror images of each other, your shaping stitches must also be mirror images of each other. Mirror counterparts are listed in the box below.*

Decreasing

Work to the desired point of decrease and then rearrange the next two DSPs so that the two stitches of the main color are next to each other and the two purls of the contrast color are next to each other. You will first decrease the knit stitches and then the purl stitches using mirror counterpart shaping moves. The same principle applies if you're working decreases with more than two stitches; you will simply have to rearrange more than two DSPs when setting up.

Increasing

With increases, no setup or rearranging is required. The trickiest part of increasing in DK is trying to avoid making large holes. Lifted increases tend to minimize the occurrence of holes.

Here's my favorite way to work a DK increase; it leaves practically no hole and looks simply lovely on both sides.

+ Note: *When picking up legs of stitches, always insert your needle tip from inside/in between layers to outside.*

Right leaning: Work up to the desired DSP, use your RH needle tip to pick up the right leg of the stitch below the next knit stitch, place it on the LH needle, and knit through the back loop with main color. Bring both yarns to the front to work the increase on the opposite side. Use the RH needle tip to pick up the closest leg of the stitch below the purl stitch of the DSP (if the opposite side were

facing you, it would be the left leg of the stitch). Put the picked-up leg up onto the LH needle (the LH needle should enter the stitch from the inside out). Purl the stitch with the contrast color. Bring both yarns to the back and slip the next knit stitch purlwise. Bring both yarns to the front and slip the next purl stitch. Increase complete.

Left leaning: Work up to the desired DSP. Slip next knit stitch purlwise, then move both yarns to the front. Slip next purl stitch, then move both yarns to the back. Use the LH needle tip to pick up the left leg of the stitch below the last knit stitch on the RH needle, and knit it through the back loop with the main color. Bring both yarns to the front. Use the LH needle to pick up the closest leg (the right leg if the opposite side were facing you) of the stitch below the last purl stitch on the RH needle. Purl the stitch with the contrast color. Increase complete.

Mirror Counterparts

M1L	⟷	M1R
LLI	⟷	RLI
k2tog	⟷	ssp
ssk	⟷	p2tog

8

CHAPTER EIGHT
brioche

BRIOCHE KNITTING IS nothing to be afraid of, but even seasoned knitters have been known to throw up their hands and mutter phrases like "I'll get around to learning that someday" and "That's on my bucket list." So how 'bout we tackle that bucket list right now?

Some parts of the brioche technique may feel familiar and some might feel completely new. There's a bit of a learning curve with all the new lingo, but the technique itself can be explained fairly simply.

When you break it down into basics, brioche knitting follows a very simple pattern of working a stitch (knitting or purling) and then slipping a stitch, repeated over and over. The new element is what you do with the working yarn when you slip stitches. In slip stitch colorwork (see Chapter Five, pages 40–45) the working yarn is held to either the front or the back of the work when you slip a stitch. In brioche the working yarn is draped over the top of the slipped stitch, like a mini shawl, essentially creating a yarn over. Those yarn overs don't get counted as separate stitches; they're buddied up with the slipped stitches and then worked together as one on the next row.

This colorwork technique is great for garments and accessories alike! It's tactile and eye-catching and ultimately really fun. So get ready to produce an incredibly squishy and lofty fabric that could be described as "ribbing on steroids"!

What You Need

Needles: With two-color brioche you really need to work with either circular needles or double-pointed needles to be successful. This is so you can slide the stitches easily from one end of the needle to the other, depending on which color you're working with. If you're working lots of increases and decreases, you should also try needles with sharp tips. (It makes it much

easier to manipulate multiple stitches.)
I also suggest using a needle a size or two smaller than you would normally use, as it will help create a more uniform look.

Yarn: In brioche knitting (just like in double knitting), no two stitches actually sit right next to each other on the finished fabric. This extra little space contributes to stitches stretching out a bit, looking wider than their stockinette counterparts. It's especially noticeable when working with slippery yarns or treated yarns (i.e., superwash yarns). An untreated yarn, such as non-superwash wool, is better at keeping its shape and helping the loose stitches stick together. That quality also comes in handy if you ever drop stitches. Whatever yarn you choose, be aware that brioche tends to eat up a lot of yarn, so you'll need quite a bit!

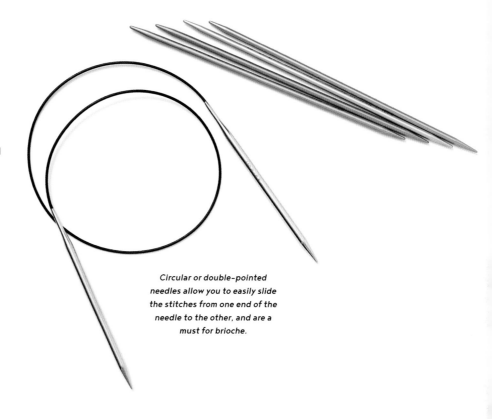

Circular or double-pointed needles allow you to easily slide the stitches from one end of the needle to the other, and are a must for brioche.

Cast-Ons and Bind-Offs

Methods for casting on and binding off are ultimately a matter of personal preference. I'll introduce you to a couple of my favorites, but know there are countless ways to start (and stop) brioche knitting, and do what works best for you. Choose a method that's loose and stretchy so that the top and bottom widths of the fabric don't cinch in excessively.

Here are my two favorite methods for casting on (see Glossary for details on how to work):

Italian two-color cast-on ❶: This cast-on is amazingly stretchy and has the appearance of just rolling out of the edge of the fabric. It can be a little fiddly and has a tendency to twist around the needle

as you work it. Make sure to straighten and align the stitches as you go. Another helpful thing to know when setting up this cast-on is to place your light/main color over your finger—and the contrast color over your thumb—and use it to make the first stitch (and last stitch if you're working flat).

Classic long tail cast-on ❷: Although the long tail cast-on isn't necessarily the stretchiest, it can be worked loosely (see the Swatch Lesson, which starts on page 78) and be a very nice candidate for brioche knitting. The reason I like this option is that it gives you a nice, clear one-color border for your brioche to "grow" out of.

❶ *Italian two-color cast-on*

❷ *Classic long tail cast-on*

Here are my three favorite methods for binding off:

Italian two-color bind-off 3 and 4:
This is also sometimes known as One-Needle Kitchener Stitch. This sewn bind-off creates the same rounded, practically invisible edge as its counterpart, the Italian Two-Color Cast-On. The bind-off should start on a right side, or light-color, row with the light side facing you. It's also a little fiddly, but worth the extra time.

Standard bind-off with preparatory row 5: I like this bind-off method because it gives the brioche fabric a clean border to top off the brioche ribs. It should be worked on a right-side row, but the color that you work it with is personal preference. I like to work my preparatory row with the dark color, so that I can then work a normal bind-off with the light color and have it match the raised ribs of the light side of the fabric. The preparatory row converts the brioche stitches back to standard stitches.

Short-cut brioche bind-off (no preparatory row) 6: Without having to work a preparatory row, this bind-off can be executed quite quickly. It is worked on a right-side row with one color only (usually with the main color). To work a short-cut bind-off, knit each brk stitch (which means knitting the stitch together with its yarn over) and purl each purl stitch (do not slip and create a yarn over) and bind-off in k1, p1 rib.

3 *Italian two-color bind-off*

4 *Italian two-color bind-off, showing the edge*

5 *Standard bind-off with preparatory row*

6 *Short-cut brioche bind-off*

Chart-Reading Must-Knows

As with other techniques, there's a lot of variation in how brioche charts look. Always refer to the key provided for detailed information.

The terminology and charting used in brioche are probably the most unfamiliar things when starting this technique. Both were largely developed by Nancy Marchant, who is a veritable guru on this topic and has published several books that I highly recommend, namely *Knitting Brioche* (2009, North Light) and *Knitting Fresh Brioche* (2014, Sixth&Spring).

As with other colorwork techniques, brioche charts show how the knitting looks on the right side of the fabric. This means that when you're working wrong-side rows, reading from left to right, you'll work the reverse of what's shown on the chart so that it turns out correctly on the right side.

Each row of brioche is worked twice, once with the light color and again with the dark color. Sometimes a chart breaks this down for you and has two Row 1s followed by two Row 2s, etc. When this is the case, each row will often be either white (to indicate the light color) or gray (to indicate the dark color).

There are basically four different types of rows that you can work when knitting brioche (or only the first two if you're knitting in the round because you're always working with the right side facing you).

LS-LC: Indicates the Light Side of the fabric being worked with the Light Color

LS-DC: Indicates the Light Side of the fabric being worked with the Dark Color

DS-LC: Indicates the Dark Side of the fabric being worked with the Light Color

DS-DC: Indicates the Dark Side of the fabric being worked with the Dark Color

Let's take a look at a few basic brioche terms. You'll see the corresponding symbol listed in front of each explanation.

Brk (often pronounced "bark"): A *brioche* knit stitch (that's what the *br* stands for). What differentiates it from a traditional knit stitch is that you're knitting a stitch together with its accompanying yarn over. As mentioned at the beginning of the chapter, the yarn over doesn't count as a stitch by itself, so this is not a decrease or k2tog but simply a brioche knit stitch.

Brp (often pronounced "burp"): A *brioche* purl stitch. Much like the brk stitch, you're purling a stitch together *with* its accompanying yarn over.

Sl1yo (slip one yarn over): This term doesn't actually mean to slip a stitch and then create a yarn over. It designates a *single* action. To work a sl1yo, always bring the yarn to the front, slip the next stitch purlwise, and then lay the working yarn over the top of that slipped stitch and work the next brk or brp.

✛ Note: *If you're working a brp next, you'll have to bring the yarn back to the front after draping it over the top of the slipped stitch. The sl1yo stitch always occurs between the brks and brps or at the beginning or end of the row.*

The other new terms you might encounter with this technique will refer to increases and decreases made with brioche stitches. For more on this topic, see the Shaping section below.

Reading Your Knitting

One of the most important things you can do as a knitter is become really comfortable with reading your work. That means being able to look at the knitting and tell if you're working a right- or wrong-side row, as well as how many rows you've knit. Here are some tips and tricks for reading brioche knitting. Two-color brioche is easier to "read" than one-color, because you can see the separate colors and the columns that they belong to.

Counting stitches: I've already mentioned that the yarn overs don't count as separate stitches. This is more visible if you spread your stitches out across the needle. By doing so, you can clearly see which stitch the yarn over belongs to and count it as "one" stitch. What looks like three loops of yarn on your needle will actually only be two stitches.

Counting rows: It can seem confusing that four rows of work only produce two rows of fabric. The easiest way to count rows is to simply count the number of knit stitches stacked on top of each other in one of the raised columns.

Calculating gauge: With gauge you need to count rows and stitches. The bigger your swatch, the easier it will be to figure out an accurate gauge. Make sure it's lying flat without any distortion and place your ruler lightly on top without pressing down too firmly. Count the number of knit ribs and purl valleys going across the work. Normal brioche gauge will have fewer stitches and more rows than stockinette knitting.

Shaping

Because brioche is always worked in pairs of stitches (sl1yos paired with brk/brps), increases and decreases happen in multiples of two (either 2, 4, or 6 stitches at a time). Increasing involves making simple, traditional yarn overs between brk or brp stitches. Decreasing can be a bit more complicated and often involves slipping stitches. Pay attention when you have to slip a stitch and make sure that, if it's a stitch accompanied by a yarn over, you slip both *together* as one. Failing to do so will leave you with an extra yarn over showing up visibly on your fabric.

Syncopation

When you syncopate brioche fabric, you change the protruding knit columns to purl valleys and vice versa. This is especially fun when working with two colors and can create really eye-popping results. To make this happen, you simply replace a brk stitch with a brp (or the other way around) and keep the sl1yos in place. You don't have to change every stitch in the row to get a great result; gorgeous patterns and shapes can be created in the fabric by syncopating small sections here or there.

Helpful Hints

Adding a new yarn: If you're attaching a new skein of the same color, try to add it somewhere in the middle of a row. Weaving in ends is very easy with brioche fabric, because there's so much loftiness between the layers. Having the ends somewhere in the middle makes them easier to hide. When attaching a new color on the edge, use a tapestry needle to bring your ends in a few stitches/columns before weaving them in.

Nervous about the next step? Putting in a lifeline before beginning a complicated section of the pattern will make it easier to rip back if you need to. Use a thinner yarn for your lifeline and pass it through each stitch currently on your needle with a tapestry needle. Lifelines are commonly placed before beginning a complicated section of a project. If you make irreparable mistakes, you can then easily rip your work back to where the lifeline was inserted and safely get all the stitches back on the needle without fear of losing any. Lifelines don't need to be removed until you're completely done with your project.

Can't remember which row comes next (or which row you just worked)? Look at the color of the yarn overs that are currently on your needle. That's the color that you just worked, so you know your next row will be in the other color. You can also look at where the loose yarn is waiting. If both colors hang on the same side, then you'll work a light-color row next; if the colors are on opposite sides then you'll work a dark-color row. The knit columns on the side facing you tell you which side you're on, the light side or the dark side. One last tip: If the color of the side facing you matches the color you're about to work with, then you'll be working brk stitches rather than brp stitches.

Brioche in the round: When working with two colors in the round, keep the yarns separate from each other. At the end of each round, bring your working yarn to the front and pick up the next color without twisting it around the other one.

Correcting Mistakes

Spotted a mistake? First, try not to panic. Before you rip out any stitches, look at where the problem lies. If the mistake is on your current row, examine the stitches around it. Look at the correct stitches to see how the two colors relate to each other, and then try to replicate that. If your answer isn't here, I recommend the Unapologetic Knitter's online tutorials on brioche (unapologeticknitter.com). They're terrific and can walk you through many sticky situations step by step.

Dropped stitch: If you drop a stitch, it's still possible to save your knitting. First, work up to the column where the dropped stitch happened and orient your work so that the color of the side facing you matches the color of the dropped stitch (it makes it easier to see what you're doing). Next, you'll have to unravel the stitches of that column one by one until you reach the dropped stitch. After you pick up the dropped stitch, rebuild your column of stitches slowly, keeping in mind that for every knit stitch you rebuild, there should be an accompanying yarn over with it.

Getting loose stitches back on the needle: Whether you have to frog (rip out) several rows or you just happened to pull the needle loose by accident, take care when picking up loose stitches in brioche. Using a needle several sizes smaller will help you get into each stitch more easily. Think of it like ribbing—you have to pick up a stitch from the back side and from the front side, in alternating order. The main difference is that the knit stitches on the side facing you will also need their accompanying yarn overs picked up with them.

Forgotten yarn over: This can be fixed on a subsequent row. The yarn over is still there, hanging out right behind the stitch that you slipped 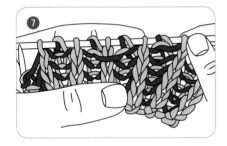. Your job is to simply ladder down to the slipped stitch, pick up the yarn over behind it, and get both back on the needle together.

SWATCH LESSON

YOU CAN CONTINUE with live stitches from another swatch lesson or choose one of the cast-on options described on page 63. if you're working this chapter as a stand-alone swatch.

In this lesson, you'll refer to the chart below as you practice a setup row, two-color brioche techniques, syncopation, and increases and decreases.

Cast on 19 sts or, since each swatch lesson in this book uses 19 sts, continue working on a previously made swatch left over from another chapter. Use the Italian two-color cast-on (see Glossary) or a long tail cast-on. Here's my trick for making the latter nice and loose: Allow a small, but even, amount of space between each stitch. I accomplish this by using my thumb and pointer finger to pinch right in

front of the most recent stitch I've cast on ❶, which prevents the next stitch I cast on from getting too close.

Row 1: Setup row. This row is important because it allows you to establish the pattern of slipped stitches and worked stitches. This swatch has an odd number of stitches. The first and last "selvedge" stitches won't be included in the brioche pattern. Knit the first stitch. The next

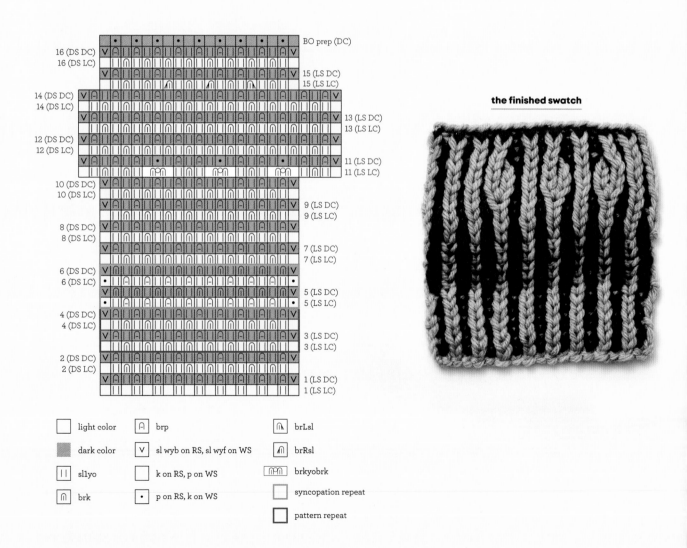

the finished swatch

	light color	A	brp	⋂	brLsl
	dark color	V	sl wyb on RS, sl wyf on WS	⋂	brRsl
‖	sl1yo		k on RS, p on WS	⋂⋅⋂	brkyobrk
⋂	brk	•	p on RS, k on WS		syncopation repeat
					pattern repeat

stitch is a "sl1yo" which you'll make by moving the yarn to the front, slipping the next stitch ❷, and then bringing the working yarn to the back by laying it over the top of the slipped stitch ❸. In a normal brioche row, the next stitch would be a brk stitch, but since you're working a setup row, you'll just use a normal knit stitch ❹. Continue alternating sl1yos and knits across the row to the last stitch, which will be the selvedge edge stitch; knit that one.

Slide all stitches back to the opposite end of the needle and get ready to work the next color. On the chart this is still Row 1, but it's being worked the second time through with the dark color (which is indicated by the row being gray). Slip the first st and then join the yarn (coming from back to front) and prepare to brioche purl or "brp" the next st and its accompanying yarn over together ❺. Next is the sl1yo, so slip the stitch ❻, bring the working yarn over the top ❼, and then bring it back to the front to work the next brp stitch. Repeat this across the row until you come to the last stitch; slip it.

Row 1 is now complete; notice that you leave the dark color on the front of the work ❽. Turn the work. Now work the dark side of the fabric, working the first part of **Row 2** (using the light color) exactly the same as the last row.

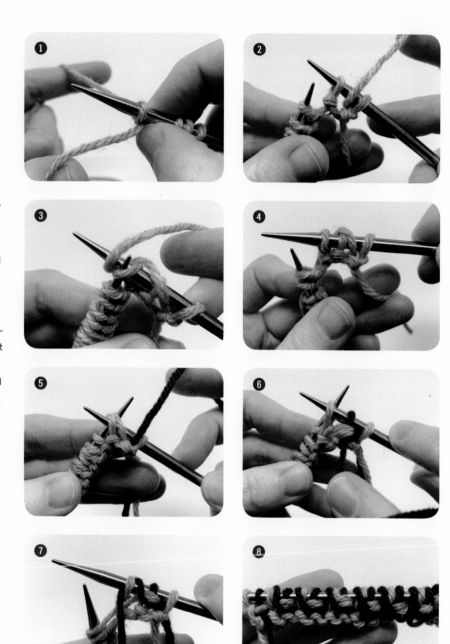

SWATCH LESSON

Your swatch looks like 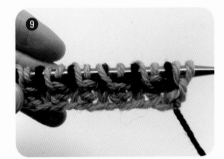 after working Row 2 (DS-LC).

Row 2 (DS-DC): Slip the first stitch and brk the next stitch on the needle (consisting of a slipped stitch with a yarn over) .

After working the brk stitch, bring the working yarn to the front to work the next sl1yo . With the yarn in front, insert your right needle tip into the next stitch and bring the working yarn over the slipped stitch and around the right needle tip to work the brk all in one movement ( and ).

At the end of Row 2, leave the dark color in the back . You've worked 4 rows now, although it looks like only 2. Work **Rows 3 and 4** as charted. Repeat these 2 rows until you feel comfortable with the rhythm of brioche and before moving on to the next step. It may take several repeats of Rows 1–4 before you see the fabric develop its signature squishy texture.

Rows 5 and 6: Time for a little syncopation. For the first row (LS-LC), purl the first stitch, sl1yo, and bring the yarn to the front to work a brp instead of a brk . It will feel weird to now brp on a nice, uniform column of brk stitches, but, trust me, this is how syncopation works! Repeat across the row, working sl1yos and brps.

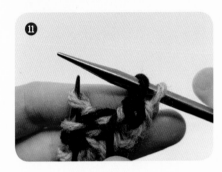 shows how the work looks after completing Row 5 (LS-LC).

Row 5 (LS-DC): The dark yarn is currently on the front of the work. Slip the first stitch , and move the yarn to the back before working the brk stitch . Work across the row in the syncopated pattern.

After completing Rows 5 and 6, you start to see how the knit and purl columns have reversed . Repeat the syncopated rows several times or until you feel comfortable with them and can see the difference in the fabric.

Rows 7–10: Return to the brioche pattern that we started with, unsyncopate your colors, and work several rows to reestablish your pattern.

Next, you'll practice increases and decreases.

Row 11 (LS-LC): On this row you'll work bkyobk increases where indicated on the chart. To do this, work up to the point of increase, make the brk stitch as usual but don't pull the stitch off the left needle , then create a yarn over  and knit into the stitch again. This increase creates 3 stitches out of 1 . Work across the row.

Row 11 (LS-DC): With the dark color, work up to the point of the increase. The first increased stitch is a sl1yo , the middle stitch should be brp stitch but it doesn't have its yarn over yet, so just work a regular purl stitch (it will get its "shawl" on the next row) and the last stitch is a sl1yo 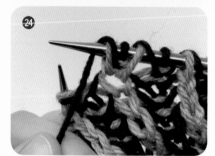.

SWATCH LESSON

Row 12: At this point you can work through the newly increased stitches with no special consideration. Work **Rows 12–14** to reestablish your brioche pattern before decreasing.

Row 15 (LS-LC): Work decreases where indicated on the chart. You'll work two different decreases, the first one leaning to the left and the second one leaning to the right; these are explained below. For the third decrease, choose either right or left leaning, depending on which one you'd like to practice again. Brioche decreases in multiples of two, so each one will take 3 stitches back down to 1.

Left leaning decrease (abbreviated brLsl): Work up to the point of decrease. Slip the next stitch and its yarn over *knitwise* **25** and **26**, and k2tog (this will look like three loops on the needle) **27**, **28**, and **29**, and pass the slipped stitch and its yarn over over the k2tog stitch **30**. **31** shows how it looks when finished.

Right leaning decrease (abbreviated brRsl): Work up to the point of decrease. Slip the next stitch and its yarn over

knitwise **32**, knit 1 st **33**, pass the slipped stitch and its yarn over over the knitted stitch **34** and **35**, and slide it back on the left needle **36**. Using your right needle tip, pick up the second stitch and its yarn over on your left needle and pass it over the top of the first stitch **37** and **38**. Slip the stitch back to your right needle. **39** shows how it looks.

Row 15 (LS-DC) and Row 16: These require no special considerations, just standard brioche knitting.

Use the dark color to work across the row in k1, p1 ribbing (knit the brks, purl the sl1yos). **+ *Note:*** *This row is a preparatory row before the standard bind-off. If you prefer the Italian Two-Color Bind-Off, you don't need to work this prep row.*

If you plan to work a swatch lesson from another chapter, stop after working your preparatory row and continue with the existing 19 stitches. Otherwise, bind off all stitches with the light color.

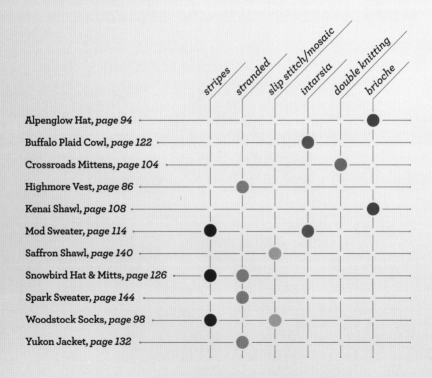

9

the patterns

If you want to practice a specific type of colorwork, refer to the chart below to select accordingly—it offers a breakdown of the techniques used in each pattern. Note that some patterns include several techniques.

	stripes	stranded	slip stitch/mosaic	intarsia	double knitting	brioche
Alpenglow Hat, *page 94*						●
Buffalo Plaid Cowl, *page 122*				●		
Crossroads Mittens, *page 104*					●	
Highmore Vest, *page 86*		●				
Kenai Shawl, *page 108*						●
Mod Sweater, *page 114*	●			●		
Saffron Shawl, *page 140*			●			
Snowbird Hat & Mitts, *page 126*	●	●				
Spark Sweater, *page 144*		●				
Woodstock Socks, *page 98*	●	●	●			
Yukon Jacket, *page 132*		●				

highmore
vest

////////////////// This gorgeous colorwork vest looks way more complicated than it really is. As with most traditional stranded colorwork, there are no more than two colors every round, and many of the rounds involve only one color. The color changes are close together so that you don't have to worry about catching floats. ¶ The pattern is worked bottom up, so that when you divide for the armholes you'll start working back and forth as opposed to in the round. Traditional Fair Isle vests are almost always steeked for the arm and neck openings, but this design has you work flat, to hone your stranded skills on the wrong side of the fabric. If you feel confident with using steeks, you can always alter the pattern; theyarnloop.com has an outstanding tutorial called Adding Steeks for Seamless Knits *that will walk you through how to convert flat patterns to be steeked.*

Finished Size

31¾ (35½, 39¼, 44¾, 48½, 52¼)" (80.5 [90, 99.5, 113.5, 123, 132.5] cm) bust circumference.

Vest shown measures 35½" (90 cm); modeled with 2½" (6.5 cm) of positive ease.

Yarn

Fingering weight (#1 Superfine)

Shown in: Anzula Luxury Fibers Dreamy (75% superwash Merino wool, 15% cashmere, 10% silk; 385 yd [352 m]/4 oz [114 g]): Storm (A) 1 (1, 1, 1, 2, 2) skein(s); Terracotta (B); One Red Shoe (C); Au Natural (D); Heidi (E); Coco (F) and Boysenberry (G), 1 skein each.

Needles

Size U.S. 1 (2.25 mm): 16" (40 cm) and 32" (80 cm) circular (cir).

Size U.S. 2 (2.75 mm): 32" (80 cm) cir.

Adjust needle sizes if necessary to obtain the correct gauge.

Notions

Markers (m); removable m; stitch holders; tapestry needle.

Gauge

30 sts and 34 rows = 4" (10 cm) in chart patt with larger needles.

Notes

✦ This vest is worked in the round from the bottom up.

✦ Stitches are bound off for the bottom of the armholes, and the front and back of the vest are worked back and forth separately.

✦ Front and back are then joined at the shoulders using Three-Needle Bind-Off (see Glossary, page 156).

✦ Finally, stitches are picked up along the armholes and around the V-neck to work ribbing.

Stitch Guide

K2, P2 Rib (multiple of 4 sts)

All rnds: *K2, p2; rep from *.

Body

With smaller cir needle and A, CO 240 (268, 296, 336, 364, 392) sts. Place marker (pm) and join in the rnd, taking care not to twist sts. Work in k2, p2 rib (see Stitch Guide) for 2¾" (7 cm).

Dec rnd: Knit and dec 2 (2, 2, 0, 0, 0) sts evenly spaced—238 (266, 294, 336, 364, 392) sts rem. Change to larger cir needle and B. Cont in St st.

Next rnd: K119 (133, 147, 168, 182, 196), pm for side, then knit to end.

Next rnd: Working row 1 of Chart A, beg at arrow for your size, k3 (10, 3, 7, 14, 7) sts from arrow to left edge of chart, work 14-st rep 16 (18, 20, 23, 25, 27) times, then work first 11 (4, 11, 7, 0, 7) sts of chart.

Work rows 2–28 of Chart A as established.

Next rnd: Working row 1 of Chart B, beg at arrow for your size and work 3 (5, 5, 3, 7, 5) sts from arrow to left edge of chart, work 8-st rep 29 (32, 36, 41, 44, 48) times, then work first 5 (3, 3, 5, 1, 3) st(s) of chart.

Work rows 2–14 of Chart B as established, and **at the same time,** on row 2 inc 2 (dec 2, inc 2, dec 0, dec 4, dec 0) sts evenly spaced, then on row 13 dec 2 (inc 2, dec 2, inc 0, inc 4, inc 0) sts evenly spaced.

✤ **Note:** Stitches are increased or de-creased to make sure the 8-st rep can be worked evenly around.

Rep rows 1–28 of Chart A, then rows 1–14 of Chart B throughout until piece measures 10½ (11, 11½, 12, 12½, 13)" (26.5 [28, 29, 30.5, 31.5, 33] cm) from CO.

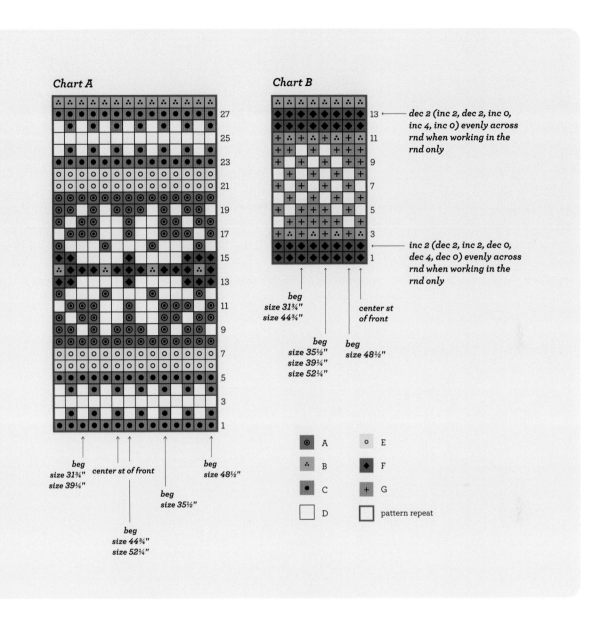

Chart A

27
25
23
21
19
17
15
13
11
9
7
5
3
1

beg
size 31¾"
size 39¼"   center st of front

beg
size 35½"

beg
size 44¾"
size 52¼"

beg
size 48½"

Chart B

13 ← dec 2 (inc 2, dec 2, inc 0,
      inc 4, inc 0) evenly across
      rnd when working in the
      rnd only
11
9
7
5
3 ← inc 2 (dec 2, inc 2, dec 0,
      dec 4, dec 0) evenly across
      rnd when working in the
      rnd only
1

beg
size 31¾"
size 44¾"

center st
of front

beg
size 35½"
size 39¼"
size 52¼"

beg
size 48½"

⊙ A   ◦ E

∴ B   ◆ F

• C   + G

☐ D   ☐ pattern repeat

ArmhoIes

✚ **Note:** If working rows 2–13 of chart B when beginning armholes, dec 2 (inc 2, dec 2, dec 0, dec 4, dec 0) sts evenly across next rnd.

Next 2 rnds: Work to last 11 (12, 14, 16, 17, 18) sts, BO next 22 (24, 28, 32, 34, 36) sts for armhole, work to 11 (12, 14, 16, 17, 18) sts before side marker, BO next 22 (24, 28, 32, 34, 36) sts for armhole, k48 (54, 59, 67, 73, 79) more sts and pm for bottom of V-neck, then work to end of rnd. Place 97 (109, 119, 136, 148, 160) sts for back on holder—97 (109, 119, 136, 148, 160) sts rem for front.

✚ **Note:** Neck shaping begins before the armhole shaping is complete; read the foll section carefully before proceeding. When working back and forth, in order to maintain the correct number of stitches for the armhole and neck shaping of both Front and Back, do not increase or decrease when working Chart B, but work neck and armhole shaping as follows.

Front

Dec row 1: (WS) Ssp, work in established patt to last 2 sts, p2tog—2 sts dec'd.

Dec row 2: (RS) K2tog, work to last 2 sts, ssk—2 sts dec'd.

Rep Dec row every row 1 (1, 5, 9, 13, 17) more time(s), then every RS row 6 (9, 8, 10, 8, 9) times. **At the same time,** when armholes measure 1" (2.5 cm), end with a RS row and beg neck shaping.

DIVIDE FOR V-NECK

Next row: (WS) Work in established patt to marker, BO 1 (1, 1, 0, 0, 0) st(s), then place rem front sts on holder.

SHAPE LEFT FRONT NECK

Dec row: (RS) Work to last 2 sts, k2tog—1 st dec'd at neck.

Cont armhole shaping and dec at neck edge as for armholes every row 13 (17, 21, 23, 23, 23) more times, every RS row 9 (11, 10, 10, 12, 14) times, then every 4 rows 6 times—10 (7, 6, 7, 9, 8) sts rem when all shaping is complete.

Work even until armhole measures 8 (8½, 9, 9½, 10, 10½)" (20.5 [21.5, 23, 24, 25.5, 26.5] cm), ending with a WS row. Place rem sts on holder.

SHAPE RIGHT FRONT NECK

Rejoin yarns and cont armhole shaping and work 1 RS row.

Dec row: (WS) Ssp, work to end of row—1 st dec'd at neck.

Rep Dec row neck edge as for armholes every row 13 (17, 21, 23, 23) more times, every RS row 9 (11, 10, 10, 12, 14) times, then every 4 rows 6 times—10 (7, 6, 7, 9, 8) sts rem when all shaping is complete.

Work even until armhole measures 8 (8½, 9, 9½, 10, 10½)" (20.5 [21.5, 23, 24, 25.5, 26.5] cm), ending with a WS row. Place rem sts on holder.

FRONT & BACK

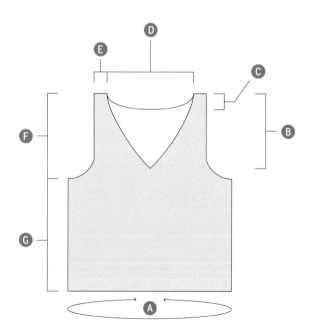

A: 31¾ (35½, 39¼, 44¾, 48½, 52¼)"
80.5 (90, 99.5, 113.5, 123, 132.5) cm

B: 7 (7½, 8, 8½, 9, 9½)"
18 (19, 20.5, 21.5, 23, 24) cm

C: 1½" (3.8 cm)

D: 7¾ (9½, 10¼, 10¾, 11¼, 11¾)"
19.5 (24, 26, 27.5, 28.5, 30) cm

E: 1¼ (1, ¾, 1, 1¼, 1)"
3.2 (2.5, 2, 2.5, 3.2, 2.5) cm

F: 8 (8½, 9, 9½, 10, 10½)"
20.5 (21.5, 23, 24, 25.5, 26.5) cm

G: 10½ (11, 11½, 12, 12½, 13)"
26.5 (28, 29, 30.5, 31.5, 33) cm

Back

Return held 97 (109, 119, 136, 148, 160) sts to larger cir needle. With RS facing, reattach yarn to right side of back.

SHAPE ARMHOLES

Dec row 1: (RS) K2tog, work to last 2 sts, ssk—2 sts dec'd.

Dec row 2: (WS) Ssp, work to last 2 sts, p2tog—2 sts dec'd.

Rep Dec row every row 1 (1, 5, 9, 13, 17) more time(s), then every RS row 6 (9, 8, 10, 8, 9) times—79 (85, 89, 94, 102, 104) sts rem.

Work even until armhole measures 6½ (7, 7½, 8, 8½, 9)" (16.5 [18, 19, 20.5, 21.5, 23] cm), ending with a WS row.

SHAPE NECK

Next row: (RS) Work 32 (29, 30, 31, 35, 34) sts in established patt, BO 15 (27, 29, 32, 32, 36) sts, then work to end—32 (29, 30, 31, 35, 34) sts rem each side.

LEFT SHOULDER

BO at beg of RS rows 8 sts 0 (0, 1, 1, 2, 2) time(s), 6 sts 3 (3, 2, 2, 1, 1) time(s), then 2 sts twice—10 (7, 6, 7, 9, 8) sts rem.

Work even until armhole measures 8 (8½, 9, 9½, 10, 10½)" (20.5 [21.5, 23, 24, 25.5, 26.5] cm), ending with a WS row. Place rem sts on holder.

RIGHT SHOULDER

With RS facing, rejoin yarns to beg with a RS row. Work 1 row even.

BO at beg of WS rows 8 sts 0 (0, 1, 1, 2, 2) time(s), 6 sts 3 (3, 2, 2, 1, 1) time(s), then 2 sts twice—10 (7, 6, 7, 9, 8) sts rem. Work even until armhole measures 8 (8½, 9, 9½, 10, 10½)" (20.5 [21.5, 23, 24, 25.5, 26.5] cm), ending with a WS row. Place sts on holder.

Finishing

Weave in ends. Block piece to measurements (see page 34). Join shoulder using Three-Needle Bind-Off method (see Glossary, page 156).

ARMHOLE EDGINGS

With smaller cir needle and RS facing, pick up and knit 148 (156, 168, 180, 184, 192) sts evenly along armhole. Pm and join in the rnd.

Work in k2, p2 rib for 1" (2.5 cm). BO all sts in patt.

Neckband

With smaller cir needle and RS facing, start at bottom of V-neck and pick up and knit 176 (196, 208, 220, 228, 240) sts evenly along left front neck, back neck, and right front neck, ending at bottom of V-neck. Do not join.

Row 1: (WS) P3, *k2, p2; rep from * to last 5 sts, k2, p3.

Row 2: (RS) K3, *p2, k2; rep from * to last 5 sts, p2, k3.

Rep last 2 rows 4 more times or until neckband measures about 1" (2.5 cm), ending with a RS row. BO all sts in patt. Sew left end of neckband to neck edge on WS and right end of neckband to neck edge on RS.

most of the colors have similar value and tend to meld visually; only the white has high contrast, making the motifs stand out.

IIIIIIIIIIIIIIIII *This hat is worked in the round from the top down. You're welcome to bind off when you get to the brim to make a beanie, but if you want to keep those ears warm, try out this little method of switching to working flat for the earflaps and then reattaching the yarn to work the brim bind-off! You (and your ears) won't regret it. ¶ Color options on this hat are really fun. You can play it restrained like my version and let the solid main color shine, or bring out the party yarn to play in front. Two contrasting colors will cause the shifting lines of the design to stand out more.*

alpenglow
hat

Finished Size

18½" (47 cm) head circumference.

Yarn

DK weight (#3 Light)

Shown in: Spun Right Round Squish DK (100% superwash Merino wool; 250 yd [229 m]/4 oz [115 g]): Snapdragon (orange, DC) and Precious (off-white, LC), 1 skein each.

Needles

Size U.S. 3 (3.25 mm): 16" (40 cm) circular (cir) and set of 4 or 5 double-pointed (dpn).

Adjust needle size if necessary to obtain the correct gauge.

Notions

Markers (m); removable m; tapestry needle; cable needle (cn).

Gauge

19½ sts and 26 rows = 4" (10 cm) in brioche rib.

Notes

✦ This hat is worked in the round from the top (crown of head) down to the brim.

✦ On the bind-off row for the brim, two sections are worked back and forth to form the earflaps.

✦ Earflaps are worked with slip stitch selvedge edges.

✦ After each earflap is completed, the yarns are reattached and the bind-off of the brim is continued.

Stitch Guide

BRIOCHE RIB (multiple of 2 sts)

✦ ***Note:*** *A brioche rnd is complete after the LC rnd and the DC rnd have both been worked as foll:*

LC rnd: *Brk, sl1yo; rep from * to end.

DC rnd: *Sl1yo, brp; rep from * to end.

Rep LC and DC rnds for patt.

Hat

Using dpn and LC, CO 10 sts, leaving an 8" (20.5 cm) tail. Distribute sts evenly over 3 or 4 dpn. Place marker (pm) and join in the rnd, taking care not to twist sts.

Next rnd: (inc) K1f&b each st—20 sts.

Brioche setup rnd 1: *K1, sl1yo; rep from * to end.

Setup rnd 2: (DC) *Sl1yo, brp; rep from * to end.

Work 1 rnd in brioche rib (see Stitch Guide).

Crown Increases

Next rnd: (inc) *Brkyobrk, sl1yo, brk, sl1yo; rep from * to end—30 sts.

Work 1 rnd even of brioche rib.

Inc Rnd 1: *Brkyobrk, [sl1yo, brk] 2 times, sl1yo; rep from * to end—40 sts.

Work 1 rnd even of brioche rib.

Inc Rnd 2: *Brkyobrk, [sl1yo, brk] 3 times, sl1yo; rep from * to end—50 sts.

Work 1 rnd even of brioche rib.

Inc Rnd 3: *Brkyobrk, [sl1yo, brk] 4 times, sl1yo; rep from * to end—60 sts.

For a Beanie (No Earflaps)

Cut LC and use DC to BO all sts using the short-cut brioche bind-off method (see page 74).

Hat with Earflaps

With LC, brk, [sl1yo, brk] 13 times (27 sts worked), pm, slip 27 sts just worked back to LH needle, with DC [sl1yo, brp] 13 times (26 sts worked) and leave the DC hanging at front of work, sl 1 from LH needle to RH needle, turn, leaving rem 63 sts of rnd unworked.

Earflap

With dpn, beg working back and forth, work next 3 brioche rows as foll:

Row 1: (WS-LC) P1, sl1yo, [brp, sl1yo] 8 times, p1—19 sts. Slide sts back to other end of needle.

Row 1: (WS-DC) Sl1, brk, [sl1yo, brk] 8 times, sl1, turn.

Row 2: (RS-LC) K1, sl1yo, [brk, sl1yo] 8 times, k1, slide sts back to other end of needle.

Row 2: (RS-DC) Sl1, brp, [sl1yo, brp] 8 times, sl1, turn.

Row 3: (WS-LC) P1, sl1yo, [brp, sl1yo] 8 times, p1, slide sts back to other end of needle.

Row 3: (WS-DC) Sl1, brk, [sl1yo, brk] 8 times, sl1, turn.

Work rows 1–11 of Chart B—5 sts rem.

Next row: (WS-LC) P2tog, brp, p2tog—3 sts rem. Cut DC.

Work 1 rnd even of brioche rib.

Inc Rnd 4: *Brkyobrk, [sl1yo, brk] 5 times, sl1yo; rep from * to end—70 sts.

Work 1 rnd even of brioche rib. Change to cir needle.

Inc Rnd 5: *Brkyobrk, [sl1yo, brk] 6 times, sl1yo; rep from * to end—80 sts.

Work 1 rnd even of brioche rib.

Inc Rnd 6: *Brkyobrk, [sl1yo, brk] 7 times, sl1yo; rep from * to end—90 sts.

Work even in brioche rib for 2½" (6.5 cm).

✛ **Note:** *Place a locking marker on a stitch from the last increase round to help you keep track of length.*

Work rows 1–13 of Chart A. Work 4 rnds of brioche rib. Piece should measure approx 7½" (19 cm).

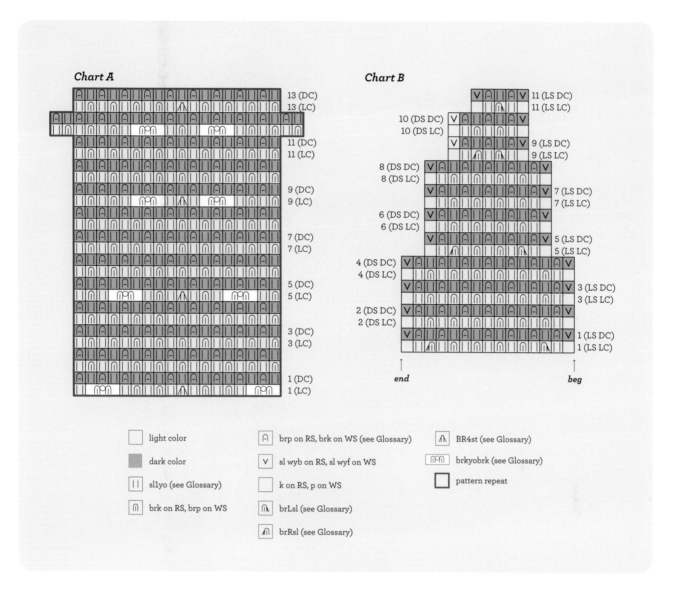

Chart A

Chart B

↑ end

↑ beg

☐ light color

▦ dark color

‖ sl1yo (see Glossary)

Ⓜ brk on RS, brp on WS

Ⓐ brp on RS, brk on WS (see Glossary)

Ⓥ sl wyb on RS, sl wyf on WS

☐ k on RS, p on WS

Ⓝ brLsl (see Glossary)

Ⓝ brRsl (see Glossary)

Ⓐ BR4st (see Glossary)

ⓂⓂⓝ brkyobrk (see Glossary)

☐ pattern repeat

I-CORD

Next row: (RS) Use LC to work 3-st I-cord (see Glossary) until cord measures approx 9" (23 cm). BO.

FRONT BO EDGE

Next row: (RS-LC) Rejoin LC to brim by picking up and knitting 1 st between last 2 sts of earflap, and place on LH needle, BO 36 sts, including st just picked up, using short-cut brioche bind-off (see page 74), [sl1yo, brk] 9 times, turn, leaving rem 17 sts unworked—19 sts.

Next row: (RS-DC) Slide sts back to other end of needle, and with dpn, join DC, sl1, brp, [sl1yo, brp] 8 times, sl1, leave DC hanging at front of work, turn.

Work same as first earflap and I-cord.

BACK BO EDGE

Next row: (RS-LC) Rejoin LC to rem sts on brim as before to pick up and knit 1 st, place that st on LH needle, BO to end. Before securing last st, pick up and knit 1 st between first 2 sts of first earflap,

BO 1, then cut yarn and pull through rem st. Fasten off so edge is smooth and sts appear continuous.

Finishing

Weave in ends. Thread CO tail through CO sts, pull tight to close hole, and pull yarn to WS. Steam block hat if desired.

woodstock
socks

///////////////// *With color blocking and stripes combined together in this simple sock design, you're almost guaranteed success with any colors you choose. It is a stash-buster's dream—feel free to add more colors or take some away and create your own color configurations! Choose high-contrast colors to make those stripes really pop, or low-contrast colors for a more subtle and subdued version. In addition to practicing your stripe colorwork, you also get a small taste of the fun you can have with slipped stitches. Occurring just on the front of the leg and the top of the foot, these slipped stitches add a quaint polka-dotted touch without diminishing the statement of the stripes!*

Finished Size

7½ (8, 9, 10¼)" (19 [20.5, 23, 26] cm) foot circumference. Socks shown measure 8" (20.5 cm) circumference.

Yarn

Fingering weight (#1 Superfine)

Shown in: Sweet Georgia Yarns Tough Love Sock (80% superwash Merino wool, 20% nylon; 425 yd [388 m]/4 oz [115 g]): Snowfall (MC), Stealth Mode (CC1), Saffron (CC2), and Tangerine (CC3), 1 skein each.

OR

Mini skeins (105 yd [96 m]/1 oz [28 g]):

MC: 2 (2, 2, 3) mini skeins; CC1: 1 (1, 2, 2) mini skein(s); CC2: 1 (1, 1, 1) mini skein; CC3: 1 (1, 2, 2) mini skein(s)

✤ *Note: CC2 uses about 10 (12, 12, 14) yd (9 [11, 11, 13] m) and could be from stash.*

Needles

Size U.S. 1 (2.25 mm): set of 5 double-pointed needles (dpn).

Adjust needle size if necessary to obtain the correct gauge.

Notions

Markers (m); tapestry needle.

Gauge

30 sts and 42 rnds = 4" (10 cm) in St st.

Notes

✤ These socks are worked in the round from the cuff down. The slip stitch pattern is designed to go across the front of the leg and the top of the foot. To customize, you can carry the slip stitch pattern all the way around the foot or choose to knit simple two-row stripes all the way around.

✤ Slip stitches purlwise with yarn in back except where indicated otherwise.

Stitch Guide

K1, P1 Rib (multiple of 2 sts)

All rnds: *K1, p1; rep from *.

Sock

With CC1, CO 56 (60, 68, 76) sts using a stretchy CO method. Distribute sts evenly over 4 dpn. Place marker (pm) and join in the rnd, taking care not to twist sts. Work in k1, p1 rib (see Stitch Guide) until cuff measures 1½" (3.8 cm) from beg.

Change to CC2, knit 1 rnd. Cont in ribbing until cuff measures 2" (5 cm) from beg.

✛ **Note:** *Knitting the first rnd of a new color before resuming ribbing avoids visible purl bumps with the color change; see Chapter Three.*

Leg

Change to MC and St st (knit every rnd). Work even until sock measures approx 3" (7.5 cm) from beg.

Work slip stitch stripe patt as foll:

Rnds 1 and 2: With CC3, knit.

Rnd 3: With MC, k27 (29, 33, 37), *sl 1, k1; rep from * to last st, sl 1.

Rnds 4 and 5: With CC3, knit.

Rnd 6: With MC, knit.

Rnds 7–18: Rep Rnds 1–6 twice more.

With MC, knit 4 (4, 5, 5) rnds.

Rep Rnds 1–18 of patt once more.

With MC, knit 4 (4, 5, 5) rnds.

Break yarns.

Heel Flap

Row 1: (RS) Join CC1, k28 (30, 34, 38), turn, leaving rem 28 (30, 34, 38) sts on separate dpn.

Row 2: (WS) Sl 1, purl to end.

Row 3: (RS) Sl 1, knit to end.

Row 4: Sl 1, purl to end.

Rep last 2 rows 9 (10, 12, 13) more times—22 (24, 28, 30) rows have been worked.

Turn Heel

Short-row 1: (RS) Knit 19 (20, 23, 26), ssk, turn.

Short-row 2: (WS) Sl 1wyf, p10 (10, 12, 14), p2tog, turn.

Short-row 3: Sl 1 wyb, k10 (10, 12, 14), ssk, turn.

Short-row 4: Sl 1 wyf, p10 (10, 12, 14), p2tog, turn.

Rep last 2 rows 6 (7, 8, 9) more times, ending with a WS row—12 (12, 14, 16) sts rem.

Next row: (RS) K6 (6, 7, 8), break CC1, pm for new beg of rnd, join MC and knit rem heel sts. ✢ *Note: This is Needle 1 to beg the gusset.*

Gusset

Setup rnd: With RS facing, use Needle 1 (N1) to pick up and knit 11 (12, 14, 15) sts in sl sts along first side of heel flap, 2 sts in gap between heel flap and instep; Needle 2 (N2), knit 14 (15, 17, 19) held instep sts; Needle 3 (N3), knit rem 14 (15, 17, 19) held instep sts; Needle 4 (N4), pick up and knit 2 sts in gap between instep sts and heel flap, 11 (12, 14, 15) sts in sl sts along second side of heel flap, then knit 6 (6, 7, 8) heel sts from N1—66 (70, 80, 88) sts, with 19 (20, 23, 25) sts each on N1 and N4, and 14 (15, 17, 19) sts each on N2 and N3.

ALTERNATE COLORWAYS

Alternate colorway (above) using Sweet Georgia Yarns Tough Love Sock in Apricot (MC), Ultraviolet (CC1), London Fog (CC2), Pumpkin (CC3)

Alternate colorway (above) using Sweet Georgia Yarns Tough Love Sock in Melon (MC), Marine (CC1), West Wind (CC2), and Basil (CC3)

Next rnd: Knit all sts, working sts picked up along the heel flap through back loops to tighten up any potential looseness.

In the following section the slip stitch pattern resumes before gusset decreasing is complete. Make sure to read through the whole section before beginning.

Dec rnd 1: N1, knit to last 3 sts, k2tog, k1; N2 and N3, knit; N4, k1, ssk, knit to end—2 sts dec'd.

Next rnd: Knit.

Rep last 2 rnds 4 (4, 5, 5) more times—56 (60, 68, 76) sts rem, with 14 (15, 17, 19) sts on every dpn.

At the same time, when gusset measures ½ (½, ¾, ¾)"/1.3 [1.3, 2, 2] cm), maintain rem gusset dec, and beg slip stitch stripe patt as foll:

Rnds 1 and 2: With CC3, knit.

Rnd 3: With MC; N1, knit; N2 and N3, [sl 1, k1] to end; N4, knit.

Rnds 4 and 5: With CC3, knit.

Rnd 6: With MC, knit.

Rnds 7–18: Rep Rnds 1–6 twice more.

With MC, knit 4 (4, 5, 5) rnds.

Rep Rnds 1–18 of patt once more.

Foot

Cont even with MC until foot measures about 1½ (1¾, 2, 2½)" (3.8 [4.5, 5, 6.5] cm) less than desired foot length. Break MC and join CC1.

Toe

Rearrange sts so that you have 14 (15, 17, 19) sts on N1; 28 (30, 34, 38) sts on N2; and 14 (15, 17, 19) sts on N3.

Dec rnd: N1, knit to last 3 sts, k2tog, k1; N2, k1, ssk, knit to last 3 sts, k2tog, k1; N3, k1, ssk, knit to end—4 sts dec'd.

Next rnd: Knit.

Rep last 2 rnds 7 (8, 9, 11) more times, then rep Dec rnd once more—20 (20, 24, 24) sts rem.

With N3, knit to end of N1—10 (10, 12, 12) sts each on N2 and N3. Cut yarn, leaving an 18" (45.5 cm) tail.

Finishing

Join rem sts using Kitchener st (see Glossary).

Weave in ends. Block using desired method (see page 34).

this design is a slight nod to a retro gym sock, complete with matching cuffs, heels, and toes and some sweet, sweet stripes.

crossroads
mittens

////////////////// *These fun, double-knit mittens are the perfect answer to the chilliest day. The two layers work together to trap air and provide extra insulation, keeping your fingers toasty. The fully reversible design gives you a couple of different looks to work with, depending on your mood, one side being more subdued and the other more colorful. If you find the small circumference challenging with double-pointed needles, try using a 9" (23 cm) circular so that you don't have to worry about constantly switching needles.* ¶ *Don't be scared off by the colorwork changes, either; remember there are no floats with double knitting, since each color is used in each pair of stitches. You'll achieve the best color outcome if MC and CC1 have the highest contrast, with a gradient of colors based on CC1.*

Size

8 (9)" (20.5 [23] cm) hand circumference, 10¼ (11½)" (26 [29] cm) long.

+ Note: *With the two layers of knit fabric, the hand circumference on the inside of these double-knit mittens is about ½" (1.3 cm) smaller than the listed size.*

Yarn

Worsted weight (#4 Medium)

Shown in: Berroco Ultra Alpaca (50% Superfine alpaca,

50% Peruvian wool; 219 yd [200 m]/3½ oz [100 g]): #6289 Charcoal Mix (MC), 2 skeins; #62100 Eiderdown (CC1), #62114 Tea Rose (CC2), #62190 Sweet Nectar Mix (CC3), #6267 Orchid (CC4), 1 skein each.

Needles

Size U.S. 3 (3.25 mm): 9" (23 cm) circular (cir) or double-pointed (dpn).

Adjust needle size if necessary to obtain the correct gauge.

Notions

Markers (m); removable m; stitch holders; tapestry needle.

Gauge

17 sts and 26½ rows = 4" (10 cm) in double-knit St st.

Notes

+ These mittens are knit seamlessly in the round from the cuff to the top of the hand.

+ The yarn is held doubled while knitting the cuff, and then the stitches are split

to establish double-knitting layers for the hand and thumb.

+ The thumb gusset is created by working increases while knitting the hand and then placing thumb stitches on scrap yarn while finishing the hand. The held stitches are then picked up and worked to complete the thumb.

+ All decreases in this pattern are left-leaning DK decreases (see page 71).

Mittens

With 2 strands of MC held tog, CO 34 (38) sts. Place marker (pm) and join in the rnd, taking care not to twist sts.

Rnd 1: *K1, p1; rep from * to end of rnd.

Rep last rnd until piece measures approx 2¾" (7 cm).

THUMB GUSSET

Inc rnd: K1f&b, work in established ribbing to end of rnd—35 (39) sts.

Break one strand of MC and join CC.

To set up for double knitting, consider each double-stranded stitch from the previous row to now be 2 separate stitches, constituting one DSP. You'll knit into the first stitch of each DSP with one strand of yarn and work the next purl stitch with the other strand of yarn.

Double knitting setup rnd: Using MC for outside sts and CC for inside sts, work 1 DSP, pm, work in DK to end of rnd.

✛ Notes: *Thumb shaping/Thumb gusset will be worked between markers. The striped column of stitches at the right edge of the chart represents the colors to be worked at the back, or inside, of each round.*

Work rows 1–18 (21) of Hand Chart and inc for thumb gusset as shown—47 (53) sts, with 34 (38) DSP for hand, and 13 (15) DSP between markers for thumb gusset. (For detailed instructions on DK increasing, see page 71.)

HAND

Next rnd: Place first 13 (15) DSP on scrap yarn for thumb gusset, work rnd 19 (22) of chart to end—34 (38) DSP rem for hand.

Work rnds 20 (23)–33 of chart. Cont with MC for outside and CC1 for inside.

Hand Chart

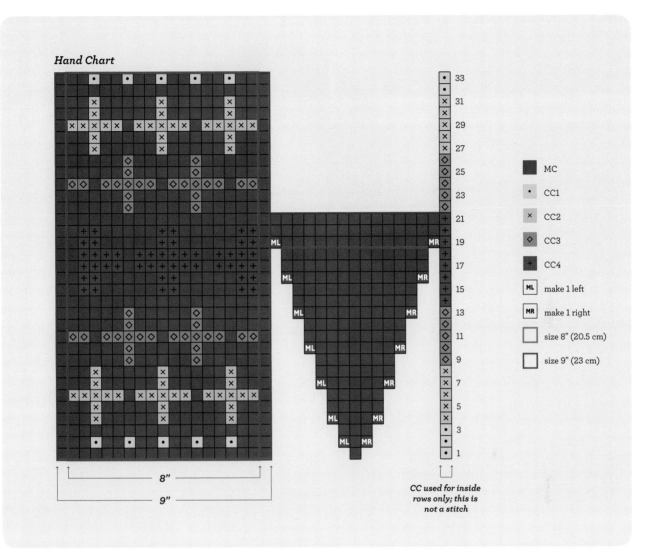

Legend	
■	MC
•	CC1
×	CC2
◇	CC3
+	CC4
ML	make 1 left
MR	make 1 right
□	size 8" (20.5 cm)
□	size 9" (23 cm)

8"

9"

CC used for inside rows only; this is not a stitch

Dec rnd (use DK dec left slanting, see Glossary): [Dec 1 DSP, work 15 (17) DSP] twice—32 (36) DSP rem.

Next rnd: *Work 8 (9) DSP, pm; rep from * to end.

Work even in DK until piece measures 8½ (9½)" (21.5 [24] cm) from CO, or approx 1¾ (2)" (4.5 [5] cm) short of desired length.

SHAPE TOP

Dec rnd: *Dec 1 DSP, work to m, sm; rep from * to end—4 DSP dec'd.

Work 1 rnd even.

Rep last 2 rnds 4 (5) more times, then rep Dec rnd once more—8 DSP rem.

Cut both strands, leaving about a 10" (25.5 cm) tail of each color. Thread tails separately through the appropriate sts (i.e., thread the gray tail through the gray sts, etc.). Working first with the inner rnd of sts, pull tight to close hole, then rep for the outer rnd of sts. Tie yarn ends together to join the two layers at the top of the hand.

Thumb

Place held 13 (15) thumb DSP on dpns, distribute sts evenly over 3 needles.

Next row: (RS) With MC for outside sts and CC4 for inside sts, beg with sts next to hand, work 1 row of DK, then with both strands held tog, pick up and k1 in gap at top of thumb gusset—14 (16) DSP. Join to work in the rnd.

Work even until thumb measures 2½ (2¾)" (6.5 [7] cm), or desired length.

SHAPE TIP

Dec rnd: [Dec 1 DSP] 7 (8) times—7 (8) DSP rem. Cut yarns and gather sts in same manner as for hand.

Finishing

Weave in ends. Block to measurements (see page 34).

kenai
shawl

////////////////// *Combining two very fun techniques, brioche and fading colors (aka ombré effect), this fun-to-wear triangular shape is worked from point to point with simple increases up the middle spine and decreases on the outer edges. ¶ I used a set of six gorgeous blues that remind me of one of my favorite places on earth, the beautiful Kenai Lake in my home state of Alaska. The turquoise shade of the water grows darker as it gets deeper, and I played with a lovely fade of those colors in this design. As far as color options are concerned, the sky's the limit. You could choose a simple pairing of two colors, one for the front side and one for the back. You could choose a set of fading colors for the front and a contrast color for the back. Or how about two sets of different fades, one for each side? Anything goes!*

Finished Size
81" (205.5 cm) long and 24" (61 cm) wide.

Yarn
Fingering weight (#1 Superfine)

Shown in: Marianated Yarns Fingering Weight Six Pack Half Skein Gradient Set in Scrumptious HT (80% superwash Merino wool, 10% cashmere, 10% nylon; 1200 yd [1097 m]/ 10½ oz [300 g]): Smooth Sailing, 1 pack.

Each pack consists of six mini skeins; each skein is 200 yd [183 m]/1¾ oz [50 g].

Label colors from light to dark, Polar Frost (A), Arctic Ice (B), Glacial Lake (C), Sea of Glass (D), Tidal Pool (E), and Jordan Pond (F).

✦ *Note: This shawl used all but 7 g, or 28 yd [25.5 m] of yarn (about 98%). Section 1 of the shawl (the increase section) takes about 70% of the yarn. To be safe, begin the decrease section when you have about 30% or 98 yd [90 m] of yarn left.*

Needles
Size U.S. 1 (2.25 mm): 24" (60 cm) circular (cir).

Adjust needle size if necessary to obtain the correct gauge.

Notions
Tapestry needle.

Gauge
21½ sts and 30 rows = 4" (10 cm) in brioche rib.

Notes
✦ This shawl is worked back and forth starting at the narrow end, working increases in the middle of rows and decreases along the edges until you reach the widest part of the shawl. At that point, half of the stitches are bound off and the remaining half are worked with decreases along both edges until all stitches are decreased.

SUGGESTED YARN SETUP

This shawl can be worked in several different ways in regards to color choice. If you choose to work with a six-color gradient set, determine which colors you want on which side of the shawl. You could easily put the three lighter colors on the front and the three darker colors on the back. I wanted to see a gradient on each side, but not the full spectrum, so I divided up my skeins and worked with a different set of five colors for each side. Preparing the yarns before beginning will make the knitting easier and allow you to move from color to color without any guesswork. Here is how I broke down the skeins:

BREAKDOWN OF 6-COLOR GRADIENT SET

	% of skein per side	
	light side	**dark side**
color A	**100%**	
color B	**60%**	**40%**
color C	**50%**	**50%**
color D	**50%**	**50%**
color E	**40%**	**60%**
color F		**100%**

For this process I recommend using a kitchen scale and setting it to grams. Weigh the full skein of yarn first and then do the math to figure out how many grams you'll need to get the right percentage. I recommend placing your newly divided skeins into two bags labeled "light side" and "dark side," so that as you reach the end of any given skein you can simply take the next darkest skein from the appropriate bag and keep knitting!

Section 1—Increase

With A and B held tog, make a slipknot and place on LH needle tip—treat as 1st CO.

Work rows 1 (LS-LC)–24 (DS-DC) of Chart A using A as the light color and B as the dark color—13 sts.

Work rows 1 (LS-LC)–12 (DS-DC) of Chart B, rep rows 5 (LS-LC)–12 (DS-DC) 36 more times, then work rows 5 (LS-LC)–8 (DS-DC) once more—165 sts.

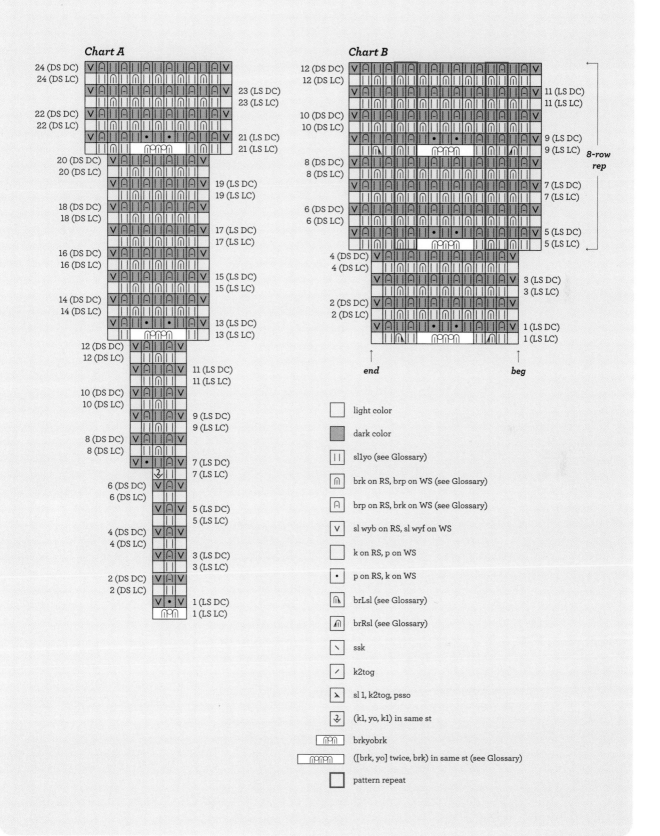

Chart A

24 (DS DC)
24 (DS LC)
23 (LS DC)
23 (LS LC)
22 (DS DC)
22 (DS LC)
21 (LS DC)
21 (LS LC)
20 (DS DC)
20 (DS LC)
19 (LS DC)
19 (LS LC)
18 (DS DC)
18 (DS LC)
17 (LS DC)
17 (LS LC)
16 (DS DC)
16 (DS LC)
15 (LS DC)
15 (LS LC)
14 (DS DC)
14 (DS LC)
13 (LS DC)
13 (LS LC)
12 (DS DC)
12 (DS LC)
11 (LS DC)
11 (LS LC)
10 (DS DC)
10 (DS LC)
9 (LS DC)
9 (LS LC)
8 (DS DC)
8 (DS LC)
7 (LS DC)
7 (LS LC)
6 (DS DC)
6 (DS LC)
5 (LS DC)
5 (LS LC)
4 (DS DC)
4 (DS LC)
3 (LS DC)
3 (LS LC)
2 (DS DC)
2 (DS LC)
1 (LS DC)
1 (LS LC)

Chart B

12 (DS DC)
12 (DS LC)
11 (LS DC)
11 (LS LC)
10 (DS DC)
10 (DS LC)
9 (LS DC)
9 (LS LC)
8 (DS DC)
8 (DS LC)
7 (LS DC)
7 (LS LC)
6 (DS DC)
6 (DS LC)
5 (LS DC)
5 (LS LC)
4 (DS DC)
4 (DS LC)
3 (LS DC)
3 (LS LC)
2 (DS DC)
2 (DS LC)
1 (LS DC)
1 (LS LC)

8-row rep

end   *beg*

light color

dark color

sl1yo (see Glossary)

brk on RS, brp on WS (see Glossary)

brp on RS, brk on WS (see Glossary)

sl wyb on RS, sl wyf on WS

k on RS, p on WS

p on RS, k on WS

brLsl (see Glossary)

brRsl (see Glossary)

ssk

k2tog

sl 1, k2tog, psso

(k1, yo, k1) in same st

brkyobrk

([brk, yo] twice, brk) in same st (see Glossary)

pattern repeat

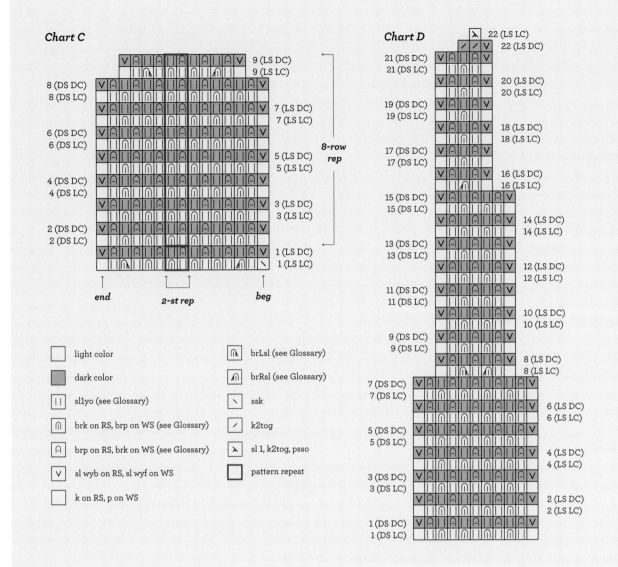

Chart C

9 (LS DC)
9 (LS LC)

8 (DS DC)
8 (DS LC)

7 (LS DC)
7 (LS LC)

6 (DS DC)
6 (DS LC)

5 (LS DC)
5 (LS LC)

4 (DS DC)
4 (DS LC)

3 (LS DC)
3 (LS LC)

2 (DS DC)
2 (DS LC)

1 (LS DC)
1 (LS LC)

8-row rep

end

2-st rep

beg

Chart D

22 (LS LC)
22 (LS DC)

21 (DS DC)
21 (DS LC)

20 (LS DC)
20 (LS LC)

19 (DS DC)
19 (DS LC)

18 (LS DC)
18 (LS LC)

17 (DS DC)
17 (DS LC)

16 (LS DC)
16 (LS LC)

15 (DS DC)
15 (DS LC)

14 (LS DC)
14 (LS LC)

13 (DS DC)
13 (DS LC)

12 (LS DC)
12 (LS LC)

11 (DS DC)
11 (DS LC)

10 (LS DC)
10 (LS LC)

9 (DS DC)
9 (DS LC)

8 (LS DC)
8 (LS LC)

7 (DS DC)
7 (DS LC)

6 (LS DC)
6 (LS LC)

5 (DS DC)
5 (DS LC)

4 (LS DC)
4 (LS LC)

3 (DS DC)
3 (DS LC)

2 (LS DC)
2 (LS LC)

1 (DS DC)
1 (DS LC)

Legend:

- light color
- dark color
- sl1yo (see Glossary)
- brk on RS, brp on WS (see Glossary)
- brp on RS, brk on WS (see Glossary)
- sl wyb on RS, sl wyf on WS
- k on RS, p on WS
- brLsl (see Glossary)
- brRsl (see Glossary)
- ssk
- k2tog
- sl 1, k2tog, psso
- pattern repeat

Section 2—Decrease

Next row: (LS) With **DC**, sl 1, p1, [brk, p1] 40 times—82 sts worked.

+ *Note: If you've altered the pattern to make it smaller or larger, simply work up to, but not including, the middle spine stitch.*

Slip sts just worked back to LH needle. With LC, loosely BO 81 sts in ribbing. Slip rem st on RH needle back to LH needle—84 sts rem.

Work rows 1 (LS-LC)–9 (LS-DC) of Chart C, then rep rows 2 (DS-LC)–9 (LS-DC) 16 more times—11 sts rem.

Work rows 1 (DS-LC)–14 (LS-LC) of Chart D. Break yarn and pull through rem st.

Finishing

Weave in ends. Lightly steam block if desired.

the turquoise
shade of Kenai Lake
grows darker as it
gets deeper, and I
imitated the lovely
fade of those colors
in this design.

mod
sweater

/////////////// *The Mod Sweater is a great piece for checking off multiple colorwork techniques. Stripes? Check. Intarsia? Got it. Carrying yarns and managing ends? Yes, indeedy. This design features color-blocking details that allow for endless color possibilities. ¶ When picking colors for this sweater, choose your stripes and background colors first, since those colors will be most prominent. Then you can play with fun, funky, and maybe unexpected colors for the accent blocks. I went with bright pink and tan as my accent colors, but you aren't limited to two. You can add more color blocks or change up where they're placed on the sweater. More information on working intarsia can be found in Chapter Six.*

Finished Size
38 (42½, 46½, 50½, 54, 56½)" (96.5 [108, 118, 128.5, 137, 143.5] cm) bust circumference. Intended to be worn with 5" (12.5 cm) positive ease.

Yarn
Worsted weight (#4 Medium)

Shown in: Cascade 220 Superwash Merino (100% superwash Merino wool; 220 yd [200 m]/3½ oz [100 g]): White #25 (A), 3 (4, 4, 5, 5, 5) skeins; Black #28 (B), 2 (2, 2, 2, 3, 3) skeins; Sugar Coral #30 (C), 1 (2, 2, 2, 2, 2) skein(s); and Doeskin Heather #40 (D), 1 skein.

Needles
Size U.S. 3 (3.25 mm): 16" (40 cm) and 32" (80 cm) circular (cir).

Size U.S. 4 (3.5 mm): 32" (80 cm) cir.

Adjust needle size if necessary to obtain the correct gauge.

Notions
Markers (m); stitch holder; tapestry needle.

Gauge
19½ sts and 29 rows = 4" (10 cm) in St st with larger needles.

Notes
✛ This sweater is worked flat in pieces and then seamed together before picking up stitches for the neckband.

Front

With A and smaller longer cir needle, CO 95 (104, 113, 125, 134, 140) sts. Do not join.

Row 1: (RS) K2, *p1, k2; rep from * to end.

Row 2: (WS) P2, *k1, p2; rep from * to end.

Rep last 2 rows until ribbing measures 2¼" (5.5 cm) from CO edge, ending with a WS row.

Change to larger cir needle and work 4 rows in St st (knit RS rows, purl WS rows).

Begin Stripe Pattern

Rows 1 and 2: Join B and work 2 rows in St st.

Row 3: (RS) Join C and k18 (19, 20, 20, 22, 22), place marker (pm), change to A and k77 (85, 93, 105, 112, 118).

Row 4: (WS) With A, p77 (85, 93, 105, 112, 118), sm, change to C and p18 (19, 20, 20, 22, 22).

Rows 5–8: Rep Rows 3 and 4 twice more.

Rep Rows 1–8 for patt, and **at the same time,** when piece measures 5½ (6¼, 6¼, 6½, 6½, 6½)" (14 [16, 16, 16.5, 16.5, 16.5] cm) from CO, end with a WS row.

SHAPE WAIST

✦ *Note: The stripe pattern is two rows of Color B alternating with six rows of Color A. Waist and bust shaping are worked within the color blocks and will not affect the line where the colors change. Color D is added while the waist/bust shaping are being worked; make sure to read the next section carefully before beginning.*

Dec row: (RS) K5, ssk, knit to last 7 sts, k2tog, k5—2 sts dec'd.

Rep Dec row every 10 (12, 12, 12, 14, 14) rows 2 more times—89 (98, 107, 119, 128, 134) sts rem. **At the same time,** when piece measures about 10" (25.5 cm) from CO, end with 2 rows in B.

Next row: (RS) With C, knit to marker, sm, join D and k12 sts, change to A, then knit to end.

Next row: (WS) With A, purl to 12 sts before marker, change to D and p12, sm, change to C, then purl to end of row.

Cont as established until piece measures 12 (12¾, 12¾, 13, 14, 14)" (30.5 [32.5, 32.5, 33, 35.5, 35.5] cm) from CO, ending with a WS row.

Inc row: (RS) K5, RLI, knit to last 5 sts, LLI, k5—2 sts inc'd.

Rep Inc row every 18 (10, 10, 16, 18, 18) rows 1 (2, 2, 1, 1, 1) more time(s)—93 (104, 113, 123, 132, 138) sts.

Work even until piece measures 16 (16¼, 16¾, 16¾, 17, 17)" (40.5 [41.5, 42.5, 42.5, 43, 43] cm) from CO, ending with a WS row.

Shape Armholes

BO 5 (5, 5, 8, 9, 10) sts at beg of next 2 rows—83 (94, 103, 107, 114, 118) sts rem.

Dec row: (RS) K1, k2tog, knit to last 3 sts, ssk, k1—2 sts dec'd.

Purl 1 WS row even.

Rep Dec row once more—79 (90, 99, 103, 110, 114) sts rem.

Work even until armholes measure 4¾ (5¼, 5¾, 6¾, 7¼, 7¾)" (12 [13.5, 14.5, 17, 18.5, 19.5] cm), ending with a WS row.

Shape Neck

Next row: (RS) K32 (37, 41, 43, 46, 47) and place these sts on holder, BO center 15 (16, 17, 17, 18, 20) sts, then knit to end—32 (37, 41, 43, 46, 47) sts rem.

Work 1 WS row even.

RIGHT SHOULDER

BO at beg of RS rows 4 sts 1 (1, 2, 2, 2, 2) time(s), 3 sts 2 (3, 2, 2, 2, 2) times, then 2 sts 1 (0, 0, 0, 0, 0) time(s)—20 (24, 27, 29, 32, 33) sts rem.

Work 1 WS row even.

Dec row: (RS) Ssk, knit to end of row—1 st dec'd.

Rep Dec row every RS row 3 more times—16 (20, 23, 25, 28, 29) sts rem.

At the same time, when armhole measures 7 (7½, 8, 9, 9½, 10)" (18 [19, 20.5, 23, 24, 25.5] cm), end with a RS row.

SHAPE SHOULDER

BO at beg of WS rows 5 (6, 7, 8, 9, 9) sts 2 (1, 1, 2, 2, 1) time(s), then 6 (7, 8, 9, 10, 10) sts 1 (2, 2, 1, 1, 2) time(s).

LEFT SHOULDER

Return held 32 (37, 41, 43, 46, 47) sts to larger cir needle. Rejoin yarn at neck edge.

BO at beg of WS rows 4 sts 1 (1, 2, 2, 2, 2) time(s), 3 sts 2 (3, 2, 2, 2, 2) times, then 2 sts 1 (0, 0, 0, 0, 0) time(s)—20 (24, 27, 29, 32, 33) sts rem.

Dec row: (RS) Knit to last 2 sts, k2tog—1 st dec'd.

Rep Dec row every RS row 3 more times—16 (20, 23, 25, 28, 29) sts rem.

FRONT & BACK

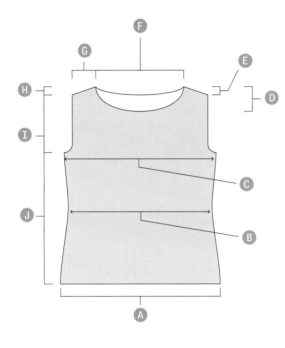

A: 19½ (21¼, 23¼, 25¾, 27½, 28¾)"
49.5 (54, 59, 65.5, 70, 73) cm

B: 18¼ (20, 22, 24½, 26¼, 27½)"
46.5 (51, 56, 62, 66.5, 70) cm

C: 19 (21¼, 23¼, 25¼, 27, 28¼)"
48.5 (54, 59, 64, 68.5, 72) cm

D: 3" (7.5 cm)

E: 1" (2.5 cm)

F: 9¾ (10¼, 10¾, 10¾, 11, 11½)"
25 (26, 27.5, 27.5, 28, 29) cm

G: 3¼ (4, 4¾, 5¼, 5¾, 6)"
8.5 (10, 12, 13.5, 14.5, 15) cm

H: ¾" (2 cm)

I: 7 (7½, 8, 9, 9½, 10)"
18 (19, 20.5, 23, 24, 25.5) cm

J: 16 (16¼, 16¾, 16¾, 17, 17)"
40.5 (41.5, 42.5, 42.5, 43, 43) cm

SLEEVE

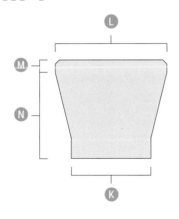

K: 9¾ (10¼, 10¾, 11½, 11½, 12)"
25 (26, 27.5, 29, 29, 30.5) cm

L: 14¼ (15¼, 16¼, 18½, 19¼, 20¼)"
36 (38.5, 41.5, 47, 49, 51.5) cm

M: 1½ (1½, 1½, 2¼, 2¼, 2½)"
3.8 (3.8, 3.8, 5.5, 5.5, 6.5) cm

N: 10¼ (10¾, 11, 10¾, 11, 11)"
26 (27.5, 28, 27.5, 28, 28) cm

At the same time, when armhole measures 7 (7½, 8, 9, 9½, 10)" (18 [19, 20.5, 23, 24, 25.5] cm), end with a WS row.

SHAPE SHOULDER

BO at beg of RS rows 5 (6, 7, 8, 9, 9) sts 2 (1, 1, 2, 2, 1) time(s), then 6 (7, 8, 9, 10, 10) sts 1 (2, 2, 1, 1, 2) time(s).

Back

With A and smaller longer cir needle, CO 95 (104, 113, 125, 134, 140) sts. Do not join.

Row 1: (RS) K2, *p1, k2; rep from * to end.

Row 2: (WS) P2, *k1, p2; rep from * to end.

Rep last 2 rows until ribbing measures 2¼" (5.5 cm) from CO edge, ending with a WS row.

Change to larger cir needle and work 4 rows in St st.

Rows 1 and 2: Join B and work 2 rows in St st.

Row 3: (RS) With A, k65 (73, 81, 92, 100, 106), change to C and k30 (31, 32, 33, 34, 34).

Row 4: (WS) With C, p30 (31, 32, 33, 34, 34), change to A and p65 (73, 81, 92, 100, 106).

Rows 5–8: Rep Rows 3 and 4 twice more.

Rep Rows 1–8 for patt. **At the same time,** when piece measures 5½ (6¼, 6¼, 6½, 6½, 6½)" (14 [16, 16, 16.5, 16.5, 16.5] cm) from CO, end with a WS row.

SHAPE WAIST

Dec row: (RS) K5, ssk, knit to last 7 sts, k2tog, k5—2 sts dec'd.

Rep Dec row every 10 (12, 12, 12, 14, 14) rows 2 times—89 (98, 107, 119, 128, 134) sts rem.

Work even until piece measures 12 (12¾, 12¾, 13, 14, 14)" (30.5 [32.5, 32.5, 33, 35.5,35.5] cm) from CO, ending with a WS row.

Inc row: (RS) K5, RLI, knit to last 5 sts, LLI, k5—2 sts inc'd.

Rep Inc row every 18 (10, 10, 16, 18, 18) rows 1 (2, 2, 1, 1) more time(s)—93 (104, 113, 123, 132, 138) sts.

Cont even until piece measures 16 (16¼, 16¾, 16¾, 17, 17)" (40.5 [41.5, 42.5, 42.5, 43, 43] cm) from CO, ending with a WS row.

SHAPE ARMHOLES

BO 5 (5, 5, 8, 9, 10) sts at beg of next 2 rows—83 (94, 103, 107, 114, 118) sts rem.

Dec row: (RS) K1, k2tog, knit to last 3 sts, ssk, k1—2 sts dec'd.

Purl 1 WS row even.

Rep Dec row once more—79 (90, 99, 103, 110, 114) sts rem. Work even until armholes measure 6¾ (7¼, 7¾, 8¾, 9¼, 9¾)" (17 [18.5, 19.5, 22, 23.5, 25] cm], ending with a WS row.

SHAPE NECK

Next row: (RS) K24 (28, 31, 33, 36, 37) and place these sts on holder, BO center 31 (34, 37, 37, 38, 40) sts, then knit to end—24 (28, 31, 33, 36, 37) sts rem.

LEFT SHOULDER

Row 1: (WS) Purl.

Row 2: (RS) BO 4 sts, work to end—20 (24, 27, 29, 32, 33) sts rem.

Row 3: BO 5 (6, 7, 8, 9, 9) sts, work to end—15 (18, 20, 21, 23, 24) sts rem.

Row 4: BO 4 sts, work to end—11 (14, 16, 17, 19, 20) sts rem.

Row 5: BO 5 (7, 8, 8, 9, 10) sts, work to end—6 (7, 8, 9, 10, 10) sts rem.

Row 6: Knit.

Row 7: BO rem sts.

RIGHT SHOULDER

Return held 24 (28, 31, 33, 36, 37) right shoulder sts to larger cir needle. Rejoin yarn at neck edge.

Row 1: (WS) BO 4 sts, work to end—20 (24, 27, 29, 32, 33) sts rem.

Row 2: (RS) Knit.

Row 3: BO 4 sts, work to end—16 (20, 23, 25, 28, 29) sts rem.

Row 4: BO 5 (6, 7, 8, 9, 9) sts, work to end—11 (14, 16, 17, 19, 20) sts rem.

Row 5: Purl.

Row 6: BO 5 (7, 8, 8, 9, 10) sts, work to end—6 (7, 8, 9, 10, 10) sts rem.

Row 7: BO rem sts.

Right Sleeve

With B and smaller shorter cir needle, CO 47 (50, 53, 56, 56, 59) sts. Do not join.

Row 1: (RS) K2, *p1, k2; rep from * to end.

Row 2: (WS) *P2, k1; rep from * to last 2 sts, p2.

Rep last 2 rows until cuff measures 2¼" (5.5 cm) from CO, ending with a RS row. Change to larger cir needle and St st. Purl 1 row.

Next row: (RS) Beg stripe patt (6 rows A, 2 rows B), and **at the same time,** beg shaping sleeve on first row as foll:

Inc row: (RS) K2, M1L, knit to last 2 sts, M1R, k2—2 sts inc'd.

Rep Inc row every 6 (6, 6, 4, 4, 4) rows 5 (4, 2, 12, 10, 9) more times, then every 4 (4, 4, 2, 2, 2) rows 5 (7, 10, 4, 8, 10) times—69 (74, 79, 90, 94, 99) sts. Work even until piece measures 11¼ (11¾, 12, 12½, 12¾, 13)" (28.5 [30, 30.5, 31.5, 32.5, 33] cm) from CO, ending with a WS row.

SHAPE CAP

Dec row: (RS) K1, ssk, knit to last 3 sts, k2tog, k1—2 sts dec'd.

Purl 1 WS row even.

Rep last 2 rows once more—65 (70, 75, 86, 90, 95) sts rem.

BO rem sts.

Left Sleeve

With B and smaller cir needle, CO 47 (50, 53, 56, 56, 59) sts. Do not join.

Row 1: (RS) K2, *p1, k2; rep from * to end.

Row 2: (WS) *P2, k1; rep from * to last 2 sts, p2.

Rep last 2 rows until cuff measures 2¼" (5.5 cm) from CO, ending with a RS row. Change to larger cir needle and St st.

Setup row: (WS) P11 (12, 13, 14, 14, 15), pm, p25 (26, 27, 28, 28, 29), pm, p11 (12, 13, 14, 14, 15).

Prepare 2 yarn supplies of color C.

Inc row: (RS) With C, k2, M1L, k9 (10, 11, 12, 12, 13), sm, with A, k25 (26, 27, 28, 28, 29), sm, with C, k9 (10, 11, 12, 12, 13), M1R, k2—2 sts inc'd.

Cont in established stripe patt (6 rows with C and A, 2 rows with B), and rep Inc row every 6 (6, 6, 4, 4 4) rows 5 (4, 2, 12, 10, 9) more times, then every 4 (4, 4, 2, 2, 2) rows 5 (7, 10, 4, 8, 10) times—69 (74, 79, 90, 94, 99) sts. Work even until piece measures 11¼ (11¾, 12, 12½, 12¾, 13)" (28.5 [30, 30.5, 31.5, 32.5, 33] cm) from CO, ending with a WS row.

SHAPE CAP

Dec row: (RS) K1, ssk, knit to last 3 sts, k2tog, k1—2 sts dec'd.

Purl 1 WS row even.

Rep last 2 rows once more—65 (70, 75, 86, 90, 95) sts rem.

BO rem sts.

Finishing

Weave in ends. Block pieces to measurements (see page 34). Sew shoulder seams. Sew sleeves into armholes. Sew sleeve and side seams.

NECKBAND

With smaller cir needle, color B, and RS facing, beg at center back neck, pick up and knit 124 (132, 136, 136, 140, 144) sts evenly along neck edge. Pm and join in the rnd.

Rnd 1: Knit.

Rnd 2: *K2, p2; rep from * around.

Rep last rnd until ribbing measures 1" (2.5 cm). BO loosely in patt.

select your
stripes and
background
colors first, then
choose fun and
maybe unexpected
colors for the
accent blocks.

buffalo plaid
cowl

////////////// *One of my favorite parts about winter is the chance to layer on the hand-knits. I love hats, mittens, and scarves in all their varieties! However, they must be functional. This cowl is knit with soft, bulky wool and is extra tall and somewhat snug fitting to ensure it actually keeps your neck warm. This pattern gives you a chance to try out simple intarsia knitting in the round. ¶ I chose a classic buffalo plaid color scheme in black, gray, and white and then threw in the green for a pop of color. You can easily change the greens to a different color family (choosing a light and dark color of another chroma), or go with an entirely different color set. To glean color inspiration, look to plaid fabric shirts or other accessories.*

Finished Size

23" (58.5 cm) circumference and 10¼" (26 cm) tall.

Yarn

Aran weight (#4 Medium)

Shown in: Quince & Co. Osprey (100% American wool; 170 yd [155 m]/3½ oz [100 g]): #102 Crow (A), #152 Kumlien's Gull (B), #126 Lichen (C), #131 Leek (D), and #101 Egret (E), 1 skein each.

Needles

Size U.S. 10 (6 mm) 24" (60 cm) circular (cir), plus an additional size 10 cir for use when finishing/grafting.

Adjust needle size if necessary to obtain the correct gauge.

✚ *Note: If you're getting more stitches to the inch with your gauge, it may be easier to work on a 16" [40 cm] circular.*

Notions

Marker (m); tapestry needle; scrap yarn for provisional cast-on.

Gauge

12½ sts and 21 rnds = 4" (10 cm) in St st.

Notes

✚ This cowl is knit in the round using the Crochet Provisional Cast-On method (see Glossary). This method is recommended over the waste-yarn method, because you'll be switching colors and attaching multiple yarn supplies in the first row of knitting, and this is more easily accomplished using the crochet cast-on.

✚ This pattern employs the yarn over technique for knitting intarsia in the round (see page 54). Other methods can be easily substituted. They can be found in Chapter Six, along with information on how to attach new yarn supplies and other relevant information for knitting intarsia.

✚ The cowl is finished by removing the provisional cast-on, placing the live stitches back on a second circular needle, and using Kitchener stitch to graft the beginning and ending edges together.

Cowl

With waste yarn, use the Crochet Provisional CO method to create a chain at least 75 chains long.

+ *Note: Each square in the plaid pattern requires approx 120" (305 cm) of yarn. Prepare yarn supplies ahead of time, measuring them to the suggested lengths.*

Row 1: (RS) Picking up sts in provisional CO and working row 1 of Plaid Chart, [k9 with A, k9 with B] 4 times, attaching a new yarn supply for each color change—72 sts. Place marker (pm) for beg of rnd, taking care not to twist sts. Turn and prepare to work intarsia in the rnd using the yarn over method (see page 54).

Row 2: (WS) Yo, work row 2 of chart and purl to last st, purl last st tog with yo made at beg of row (this essentially joins the work in the rnd to make sure the sts are not twisted before joining), turn.

Next row: (RS) Yo, work next row of chart and knit to last st, ssk last st tog with yo made at beg of the row, turn.

Next row: (WS) Yo, work next row of chart and purl to last st, purl last st tog with yo made at beg of row, turn.

Work rows 5–36 of chart by repeating the last 2 rows, then rep rows 1–36 two more times.

+ *Note: Each square is made up of 9 sts and 12 rows.*

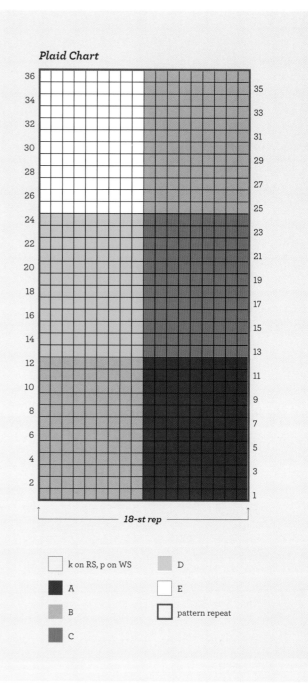

Plaid Chart

18-st rep

- k on RS, p on WS
- A
- B
- C
- D
- E
- pattern repeat

Finishing

Remove provisional CO and place resulting live sts on separate cir needle. Fold cowl in on itself so that last row you worked is lined up with first row. With B, join ends using Kitchener st (see Glossary).

Weave in ends. Block using desired method (see page 34).

snowbird
hat & mitts

////////////// *The Snowbird Hat & Mitts are both great patterns to test out your stranded color-work skills. They're small, portable projects that pack a big, colorful punch. With seven different colors, these pieces throw open the door of color options and give you the chance to play with dominant and recessive colors. Try choosing two or three colors that work well together (see Chapter One: Understanding Color) and then as the remaining colors pick either tints and shades of the main colors, or possibly their analogous colors. These accessories work up quickly and make a perfect addition to fall, winter, and spring wardrobes!*

Finished Size

Hat: 18½ (20½)" (47 [52] cm) circumference above brim; 12" (30.5 cm) tall with brim unfolded.

Mitts: 6¾ (7½, 8¼)" (17 [19, 21] cm) hand circumference and 7 (7½, 7¾)" (18, 19, 19.5] cm) tall.

Yarn

Worsted weight (#4 Medium)

Shown in: Hazel Knits Cadence (100% superwash Merino wool; 200 yd [183 m]/3⅞ oz

[110 g]): Collegiate (navy, A), Silica (beige, B), Stick O'Butter (bright yellow, C), Hoppy Blonde (gold, D), Jam Session (burgundy, E), Ruby Love (red, F), and Zest (dark orange, G), 1 skein each for Hat or Mitts. **✦ Note:** *If making both pieces, 1 skein of A should be enough to make both hat and mitts, and 1 skein each of colors B–G will make both pieces.*

Needles

Size U.S. 3 (3.25 mm): 16" (40 cm) circular (cir)

and set of 4 or 5 double-pointed (dpn).

Size U.S. 5 (3.75 mm): 16" (40.5 cm) cir and set of 4 or 5 dpn.

Adjust needle sizes if necessary to obtain the correct gauge.

Notions

Markers (m); waste yarn; tapestry needle; 2–3" (5–7.5 cm) pompom maker.

Gauge

23½ sts and 26 rnds = 4" (10 cm) in chart patt with larger needles.

Notes

✦ This hat is worked in the round from the brim up.

✦ The mitts are worked in the round from the cuff up. The colorwork pattern is fully charted and includes a traditional thumb gusset.

Stitch Guide

Twisted Rib (multiple of 2)

All rnds: *K1-tbl, p1; rep from * to end.

Hat

With smaller cir needle and A, CO 108 (114) sts. Place marker (pm) and join in the rnd, taking care not to twist sts. Work 3" (7.5 cm) of Twisted Rib (see Stitch Guide).

Size 20½" (52 cm) Only

Inc rnd: [K18, k1f&b] 6 times—120 sts.

Both Sizes

Change to larger cir needle.

Work ¾" (2 cm) in St st (knit every rnd).

Work rows 1–53 (54) of Chart A (B)—12 sts rem. Change to dpn when there are too few sts to work comfortably on cir needle.

Break yarn, leaving an 8" (20.5 cm) tail. Thread tail through rem sts, pull tight to close and secure on WS.

Finishing

Weave in ends. Block to measurements (see page 34). **✦ Note:** *If you intend to turn up the brim for regular wear, weave in the CO tail on the RS so it's hidden when the brim is folded up.*

Using A, make a pompom and attach to top of hat.

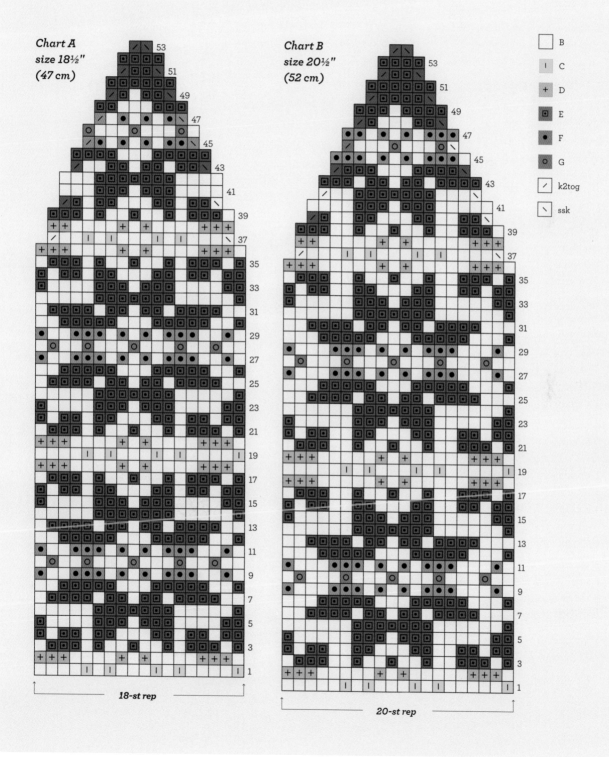

Chart A
size 18½"
(47 cm)

Chart B
size 20½"
(52 cm)

18-st rep

20-st rep

	B
	C
	D
	E
	F
	G
	k2tog
	ssk

Mitts

With smaller dpn and A, CO 40 (44, 48) sts. Place marker (pm) and join in the rnd, taking care not to twist sts. Work 2¾" (7 cm) of Twisted Rib (see Stitch Guide).

Change to larger dpn and E. Knit 2 rnds.

THUMB GUSSET

Setup rnd: K20 (22, 24), pm, M1L, pm, knit to end—41 (45, 49) sts, with 20 (22, 24) sts each for palm and back of hand, and 1 st for thumb gusset.

LEFT MITT

Next rnd: Working rnd 1 of charts, work Palm Chart over 20 (22, 24) sts as foll: work 0 (1, 0) st(s) at right edge of chart, 4-st rep 5 (5, 6) times, then 0 (1, 0) st(s) at left edge of chart, sm, work Thumb Gusset Chart for your size over next st, sm, then work Star Chart over rem 20 (22, 24) sts.

RIGHT MITT

Next rnd: Working rnd 1 of charts, work Star Chart over 20 (22, 24) sts, sm, work Thumb Gusset Chart for your size over next st, sm, then work Palm Chart over rem 20 (22, 24) sts as foll: work 0 (1, 0) st(s) at right edge of chart, 4-st rep 5 (5, 6) times, then 0 (1, 0) st(s) at left edge of chart.

BOTH MITTS

Work rows 2–15 of charts as established—53 (59, 63) sts, with 40 (44, 48) sts for hand and 13 (15, 15) sts for thumb gusset.

HAND

Next rnd: With E, knit to gusset marker, place next 13 (15, 15) sts on scrap yarn for thumb, then knit to end—40 (44, 48) sts rem for hand.

Knit 2 rnds even.

Change to smaller dpn and A. Knit 1 (3, 5) rnd(s).

Work 1¼" (3.2 cm) of Twisted Rib, or to desired hand length. BO in patt.

Thumb

Place held thumb sts on smaller dpn.

With A, k13 (15, 15) sts, then pick up and knit 3 sts in gap at top of opening—16 (18, 18) sts. Pm and join in the rnd.

Work 1¼" (3.2 cm) of Twisted Rib. BO in patt.

Finishing

Weave in ends. Block to measurements (see page 34).

MITT CHARTS

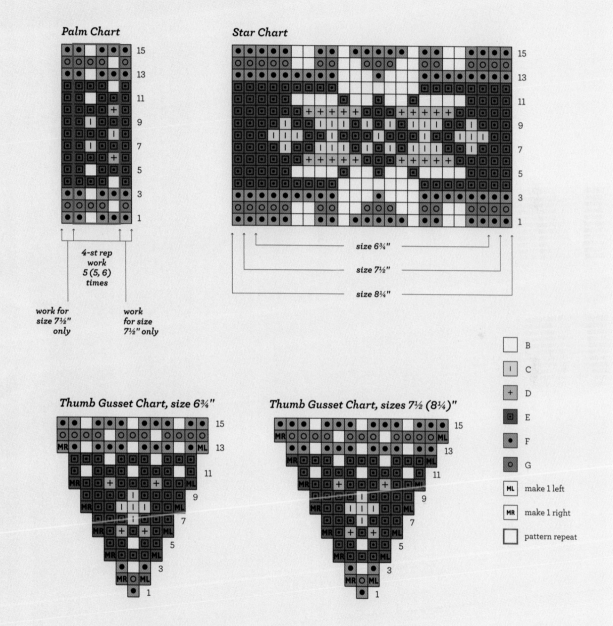

Palm Chart

4-st rep work 5 (5, 6) times

work for size 7½" only

work for size 7½" only

Star Chart

size 6¾"

size 7½"

size 8¼"

Thumb Gusset Chart, size 6¾"

Thumb Gusset Chart, sizes 7½ (8¼)"

	B
I	C
+	D
▣	E
●	F
○	G
ML	make 1 left
MR	make 1 right
	pattern repeat

yukon
jacket

//////////////// This jacket's chunky wool and flattering silhouette are perfect for the cool days of fall or winter, depending on where you live! Color possibilities are endless with a traditional colorwork yoke like this one. You can play with a darker body color and a lighter yoke or mix up the placement of the high-contrast colors (the yellow and the mint) to get a completely different look. The "lice" pattern (single spaced stitches in a contrasting color) on the body and sleeves can be omitted, as well as the pockets. This jacket is knit in the round from the bottom up and steeked upon completion. After cutting the steek, stitches are picked up on the front edges to create the button bands. The pockets are added afterward, if desired—but who says no to pockets?!

Finished Size

35¼ (38½, 43¼, 46½, 51¼, 53)" (89.5 (98, 110, 118, 130, 134.5] cm) bust circumference, buttoned.

Cardigan shown measures 38½" (98 cm), modeled with 5½" (14 cm) of positive ease.

Yarn

Chunky weight (#5 Bulky)

Shown in: Malabrigo Chunky (100% Merino wool; 104 yd [95 m]/3½ oz [100 g]): #CH073 Uva (purple, A), 2 (2, 2, 3, 3, 3) skeins; #CH083 Water Green (light green, B), 1 (1, 1, 1, 2, 2) skein(s); #CH150 Azul Profundo (navy, C), 2 (2, 2, 3, 3, 3) skeins; #CH035 Frank Ochre (gold, D), 1 (1, 2, 2, 2, 2) skein(s); #CH036 Pearl (light gray, E), 4 (5, 5, 6, 6, 7) skeins; #CH063 Natural (white, F), 1 (1, 2, 2, 2, 2) skein(s); #CH019 Pollen (yellow, G), 1 skein.

Needles

Size U.S. 6 (4 mm): 16" (40 cm) and 32" (80 cm) circular and set of 4 or 5 double-pointed (dpn).

Size U.S. 8 (5 mm): 16" (40 cm), 24" (60 cm) and 32" (80 cm) cir and set of 4 or 5 dpn.

Adjust needle size if necessary to obtain the correct gauge.

Notions

Markers (m); stitch holders or waste yarn; tapestry needle; six 1⅛" (28 mm) buttons; 5" by 27" (12.5 cm by 68.5 cm) fabric for facings; matching sewing thread.

Gauge

15 sts and 19 rows = 4" (10 cm) in chart patt with larger needles.

Notes

✦ This cardigan is worked in the round from the bottom up with a 7-stitch steek up the center front.

✦ The sleeves are worked separately in the round and then joined to the body before completing the yoke.

✦ To work nearly invisible increases with this chunky-weight yarn, I recommend using the BL-left and BL-right increases (see Glossary); however, you can use whatever increase method you prefer.

✦ The collar is worked back and forth in ribbing after the yoke has been completed.

✦ Once the garment is finished, the steek is cut, opening up the front of the cardigan, and button bands are picked up and knit along the front edges.

✦ Pockets are worked separately, then sewn on after the body is complete.

Stitch Guide

3-row Buttonhole (worked over 2 knit sts in k2, p2, rib)

Row 1: (WS) K1, yo, k1—3 sts.

Row 2: (RS) P3.

Row 3: K1, k2tog—2 sts.

Sleeves (make 2)

With smaller dpn and A, CO 28 (32, 32, 36, 40, 40) sts. Place marker (pm) and join in the rnd, taking care not to twist sts. Work in k2, p2 rib (see page 87) for 3" (7.5 cm).

Change to larger dpn and B. Cont in St st (knit every rnd).

Inc rnd: Knit and inc 2 (4, 4, 0, 2, 2) sts evenly spaced—30 (36, 36, 36, 42, 42) sts.

Work rows 1–6 of Chart A, working 6-st rep only.

Inc rnd: Working row 1 of Chart B, and with E, k1, BL-left, work to last st, BL-right, k1—2 sts inc'd. **+Note:** *Make sure single sts in color F are centered over chart A patt.*

Work rows 2–6 of chart, then rep rows 1–6, and **at the same time,** rep Inc rnd every 8 (12, 8, 6, 6, 6) rnds 7 (2, 3, 7, 7, 3) more times, then every 0 (10, 6, 4, 4, 4) rnds 0 (3, 6, 5, 5, 11) times—46 (48, 56, 62, 68, 72) sts.

Cont even until piece measures 18 (18, 18½, 18½, 19, 19)" (45.5 [45.5, 47, 47, 48.5, 48.5] cm) from CO, ending with row 1 or 4 of chart.

Slip first 5 (6, 7, 7, 8, 8) sts and last 5 (6, 7, 7, 8, 8) sts to holder or waste yarn—36 (36, 42, 48, 52, 56) sts rem. Set aside.

Body

With smaller cir needle and A, CO 129 (145, 161, 173, 189, 197) sts. Pm and join in the rnd, taking care not to twist sts.

Next rnd: K4, pm for steek, work in k2, p2 rib to last 5 sts, k2, pm for steek, k3.

Work steek sts in St st over the 7 sts between steek markers, and k2, p2 ribbing over rem sts until piece measures 2¼" (5.5 cm) from CO.

Change to larger cir needle and B.

Inc rnd: Knit and inc 5 (1, 3, 3, 5, 3) st(s) evenly spaced; do not work any inc between steek markers—134 (146, 164, 176, 194, 200) sts.

Next rnd: Work 4 steek sts, sm, working row 1 of Chart A, work 6-st rep to 1 st before steek marker, work 1 st at left edge of chart, sm, work 3 steek sts.

Work rows 2–6 of chart.

Next rnd: With E only, knit.

Next rnd: Work 4 steek sts, sm, working row 1 of Chart B, work 6-st rep to 1 st before steek marker, work 1 st at left edge of chart, sm, work 3 steek sts.

Work rows 2–6 of Chart B, then rep rows 1–6 until piece measures 13¼ (13½, 13½, 13½, 14, 14½)" (33.5 [34.5, 34.5, 34.5, 35.5, 37] cm) from CO, ending with row 1 or 4 of chart.

Yoke

Joining rnd: With E only, k31 (33, 36, 39, 43, 44) body sts for left front (including 4 steek sts), place next 10 (12, 14, 14, 16, 16) sts on holder for underarm, k36 (36, 42, 48, 52, 56) held sleeve sts, k53 (57, 65, 71, 77, 81) body sts for back, place next 10 (12, 14, 14, 16, 16) sts on holder for underarm, k36 (36, 42, 48, 52, 56) held sleeve sts, then k30 (32, 35, 38, 42, 43) rem sts for right front (including 3 steek sts)—186 (194, 220, 244, 266, 280) sts.

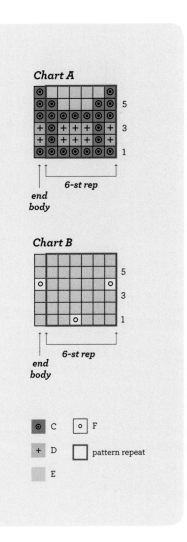

Chart A

6-st rep

end body

Chart B

6-st rep

end body

◉ C   ◦ F

+ D   ☐ pattern repeat

E

Next rnd: Knit and inc 0 (inc 4, inc 2, inc 2, dec 2, inc 2) sts evenly spaced—186 (198, 222, 246, 264, 282) sts.

+Note: *It's a good idea to increase or decrease where the sleeves join the body.*

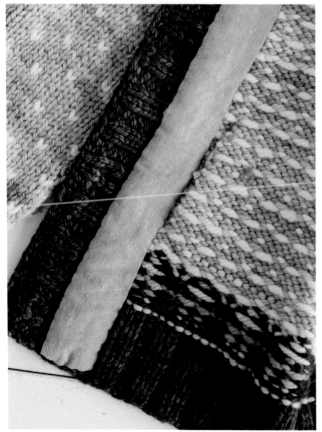

Next rnd: Work 4 steek sts as established, sm, work 6-st rep of row 1 Chart C (C, C, D, D, D) to 5 sts before steek marker, work 5 sts at left edge of chart, sm, then work 3 steek sts.

Work rows 2–24 (24, 24, 29, 29, 29) of Chart C (C, C, C, D, D, D)—126 (134, 150, 166, 178, 190) sts rem. Change to shorter larger cir needle when too few sts rem to work comfortably on longer cir needle.

Next rnd: With C only, knit.

Dec rnd: Knit steek sts, sm, *k2tog, k2; rep from * to 3 sts before steek marker, k2tog, k1, sm, knit steek sts—96 (102, 114, 126, 135, 144) sts rem.

Work 0 (1, 3, 1, 2, 2) rnd(s) even.

SHAPE NECK

✦ *Note: Steek sts are included in st counts.*

Short-row 1: (RS) K84 (89, 99, 110, 117, 125) sts, w&t.

Short-row 2: (WS) P73 (77, 85, 95, 100, 107) sts, w&t.

Short-row 3: K67 (71, 79, 89, 94, 101) sts, w&t.

Short-row 4: P61 (65, 73, 83, 88, 95) sts, w&t.

Short-row 5: K55 (59, 67, 77, 82, 89) sts, w&t.

Short-row 6: P49 (53, 61, 71, 76, 83) sts, w&t.

Short-row 7: Knit to end of rnd, picking up wraps.

Work 1 (3, 3, 1, 1, 1) rnd(s) even, picking up rem wraps.

✦ *Note: The following decrease instructions include the steek stitches in the st counts for all sizes.*

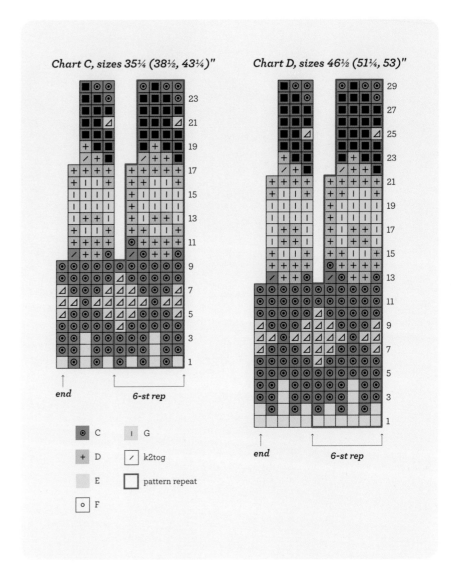

Chart C, sizes 35¼ (38½, 43¼)"

Chart D, sizes 46½ (51¼, 53)"

end   6-st rep

end   6-st rep

⊙	C		I	G
+	D		∕	k2tog
	E		☐	pattern repeat
○	F			

For Sizes 35¼ (38½, 43¼)" (89.5 [98, 110] cm) Only

Dec rnd: K5, k2tog, *k1, k2tog; rep from * to last 5 sts, k2tog, k3—66 (70, 78) sts rem.

Knit 1 rnd even.

Dec rnd: K8 (7, 10), k2tog, [k4 (5, 5), k2tog] 8 times, k6 (3, 8), removing steek marker, 2 sts rem unworked at end of rnd—57 (61, 69) sts rem.

For Size 46½" (118 cm) Only

Dec rnd: K9, [k2tog, k3] 22 times, k7—104 sts rem.

Knit 2 rnds even.

Dec rnd: K9, [k2tog, k2] 22 times, k7—82 sts rem.

Knit 1 rnd even.

Dec rnd: K9, k2tog, [k6, k2tog] 8 times, k5, removing steek marker, 2 sts rem unworked at end of rnd—73 sts rem.

For Size 51¼" (130 cm) Only

Dec rnd: K5, [k2tog, k3] 10 times, [k2tog, k2] 6 times, [k2tog, k3] 10 times, k2tog, k4—108 sts rem.

Knit 2 rnds even.

Dec rnd: K4, [k2tog, k2] 10 times, [k2tog, k1] 6 times, [k2tog, k2] 10 times, k2tog, k4—81 sts rem.

Knit 1 rnd even.

Dec rnd: [K7, k2tog] 8 times, k7, removing steek marker, 2 sts rem unworked at end of rnd—73 sts rem.

For Size 53" (134.5 cm) Only

Dec rnd: K5, [k2tog, k2] 9 times, [k2tog, k3] 13 times, [k2tog, k2] 8 times, k2tog, k4—113 sts rem.

Knit 3 rnds even.

Dec rnd: K4, [k2tog, k1] 9 times, [k2tog, k2] 13 times, [k2tog, k1] 8 times, k2tog, k4—82 sts rem.

Knit 1 rnd even.

Dec rnd: K9, k2tog, [k6, k2tog] 8 times, k5, removing steek marker, 2 sts rem unworked at end of rnd—73 sts rem.

All Sizes
Collar

Change to shorter smaller cir needle.

Next rnd: BO 4 sts (last 2 sts from end of last rnd and first 2 sts from beg of next rnd) and remove beg-of-rnd marker, slip last st from RH needle back to LH needle, k2tog, remove steek marker, *k2, p2; rep from * to last 3 sts, k3—52 (56, 64, 68, 68, 68) sts rem.

Cont working back and forth.

Next row: (WS) P3, *k2, p2; rep from * to last 5 sts, k2, p3.

Next row: (RS) K3, *p2, k2; rep from * to last 5 sts, p2, k3.

Rep last 2 rows until ribbing measures 2½" (6.5 cm), ending with a RS row.

BO all sts in patt.

Finishing & Steeking

Weave in ends. Join underarm sts using Kitchener stitch (see page 154). Block pieces to measurements (see page 34).

Machine stitch reinforcement seams on either side of the center steek stitch, as shown in ❶.

+ Note: It's possible to reinforce the steek with hand stitching, but when working with a bulkier yarn weight such as this, I recommend machine stitching if at all possible.

After sewing the steek reinforcements, carefully cut the steek open along the center using a pair of sharp scissors ❷.

BUTTON BAND

With longer smaller cir needle and RS facing, use A to pick up and knit 80 (88, 88, 88, 92, 92) sts evenly along left front edge of steek from top of collar down to CO edge. Do not join.

+ Note: Make sure to pick up stitches so reinforcement stitching is between cut edge of steek and stitches picked up.

Row 1: (WS) P3, k2, *p2, k2; rep from * to last 3 sts, p3.

Row 2: (RS) K3, p2, *k2, p2; rep from * to last 3 sts, k3.

Rep last 2 rows until button band measures 1½" (3.8 cm), ending with a RS row.

BO all sts in rib.

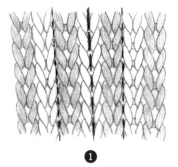

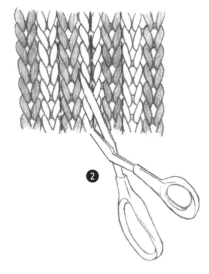

FRONT & BACK

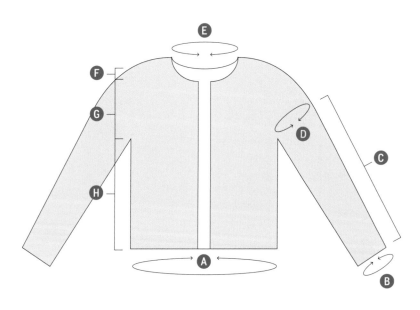

A: 33¾ (37, 41¾, 45, 49¾, 51½)"
85.5 (94, 106, 114.5, 126.5, 131) cm
not including front bands or steek

B: 8 (9½, 9½, 9½, 11¼, 11¼)"
20.5 (24, 24, 24, 28.5, 28.5) cm

C: 18 (18, 18½, 18½, 19, 19)"
45.5 (45.5, 47, 47, 48.5, 48.5) cm

D: 12¼ (12¾, 15, 16½, 18¼, 19¼)"
31 (32.5, 38, 42, 46.5, 49) cm

E: 13¾ (15, 17, 18¼, 18¼, 18¼)"
35 (38, 43, 46.5, 46.5, 46.5) cm
not including front bands or steek

F: 1½" (3.8 cm)

G: 6¾ (7¼, 7¾, 8¾, 8¾, 9)"
17 (18.5, 19.5, 22, 22, 23) cm

H: 13¼ (13½, 13½, 13½, 14, 14½)"
33.5 (34.5, 34.5, 34.5, 35.5, 37) cm

BUTTONHOLE BAND

With longer smaller cir needle and RS facing, use A to pick up and knit 80 (88, 88, 88, 92, 92) sts evenly along right front edge of steek from CO edge to top of collar. Do not join.

Row 1: (WS) P3, k2, *p2, k2; rep from * to last 3 sts, p3.

Row 2: (RS) K3, p2, *k2, p2; rep from * to last 3 sts, k3.

For Size 35¼" (89.5 cm) Only

Buttonhole row: P3, work row 1 of buttonhole over next 2 sts (see Stitch Guide), p2, k2, p2, make buttonhole over next 2 sts, *p2, [k2, p2] 3 times, make buttonhole over next 2 sts; rep from * 3 more times, p3—86 sts.

For Sizes 38½ (43¼, 46½)" (98 [110, 118] cm) Only

Buttonhole row: P3, k2, p2, work row 1 of buttonhole over next 2 sts (see Stitch Guide), p2, [k2, p2] twice, make buttonhole over next 2 sts, *p2, [k2, p2] 3 times, make buttonhole over next 2 sts; rep from * 3 more times, p3—94 sts.

For Sizes 51¼ (53)" (130 [134.5] cm) Only

Buttonhole row: P3, k2, p2, work row 1 of buttonhole over next 2 sts (see Stitch Guide), *p2, [k2, p2] 3 times, make buttonhole over next 2 sts; rep from * 4 more times, p3—98 sts.

All Sizes

Row 4: (RS) Working in established ribbing, purl all yo's as for row 2 of 3-row Buttonhole (see Stitch Guide).

Row 5: (WS) Work in ribbing and work row 3 of 3-row Buttonhole—80 (88, 88, 88, 92, 92) sts rem.

Row 6: (RS) K3, p2, *k2, p2; rep from * to last 3 sts, k3.

Work in established ribbing for 2 more rows. BO all sts in rib.

Cut fabric for facings into two pieces, each 2½" (6.5 cm) wide and 1" (2.5 cm) longer than steeks. Fold under ½" (1.3 cm) along all edges of both facings. Trim steeks to about 2 sts wide, then fold toward body. Pin facings to body, covering cut edges of steeks. Sew each facing to front edges, covering steek cut edges (see detail photo on page 135, bottom left).

Sew buttons to button band opposite buttonholes.

POCKETS (OPTIONAL, MAKE 2)

With shortest larger cir needle and E, CO 13 sts.

Inc row 1: (WS) P1f&b, purl to last st, p1f&b—2 sts inc'd.

Inc row 2: (RS) K1f&b, knit to last st, k1f&b—2 sts inc'd.

Rep Inc row 1 once more—19 sts.

Work rows 1–11 of Pocket Chart. Change to C and purl 1 row.

Change to shorter smaller cir needle.

Row 1: (RS) *K2, p2; rep from * to last 3 sts, k3.

Row 2: (WS) P3, *k2, p2; rep from * to end.

Work in established ribbing for 4 more rows. BO all sts in patt.

Weave in ends. Sew pockets to front of jacket as shown in photo, facing page.

Pocket Chart

Legend:
⊿ B
+ D
(shaded) E
○ F

saffron
shawl

////////////// This striking rectangular shawl is the perfect piece to test out your mosaic knitting skills on. Knitting flat back and forth—with only one color at a time—you will get to practice slipping stitches on the right side of the work as well as the wrong side. When choosing colors for this design, keep in mind the importance of color value. Since you're repeating a relatively small motif over and over again, make sure to pick two colors that have very different values and therefore very strong contrast.

Finished Size

16¾" (42.5 cm) wide and 70" (178 cm) long.

Yarn

Fingering weight (#1 Superfine)

Shown in: The Plucky Knitter Primo Fingering (75% Merino wool, 20% cashmere, 5% nylon; 400 yd [366 m]/4 oz [115 g]): I Sea You (MC), 2 skeins; Slug Bug (CC), 2 skeins.

Needles

Size U.S. 3 (3.25 mm): straight, 16" (40 cm) or 24" (60 cm) circular (cir).

Adjust needle size if necessary to obtain the correct gauge.

Notions

Tapestry needle.

Gauge

27 sts and 54 rows = 4" (10 cm) in mosaic patt.

Notes

✦ This rectangular shawl is worked back and forth.

✦ Working the mosaic chart the recommended number of times will yield a shawl about 70" (178 cm) long. To shorten or lengthen it, simply change the number of chart repeats.

✦ You can also change the number of cast-on stitches to work a wider or narrower shawl. If you make changes to the width, be sure to add or subtract multiples of 10 so the total number of stitches cast on is a multiple of 10 stitches plus 3.

✦ For information and tips on how to read the mosaic chart or work neat selvedge edges, see Chapter Five.

Shawl

With MC, CO 113 sts.

Knit 2 rows.

Change to CC, knit 2 rows.

Next row: (RS, MC) *K1, sl 1 wyb; rep from * to last st, k1.

Next row: (WS, MC) *K1, sl 1 wyf; rep from * to last st, k1.

Next row: (RS, CC) K2, *sl 1 wyb, k1; rep from * to last st, k1.

Next row: (WS, CC) K1 *p1, sl 1 wyf; rep from * to last 2 sts, p1, k1.

Knit 2 rows with MC.

Work rows 1–32 of Saffron Chart 29 times or until approx ¾" (2 cm) short of desired length. Piece should measure approx 69¼" (176 cm) from beg.

Knit 2 rows with MC.

Next row: (RS, CC) *K1, sl 1 wyb; rep from * to last st, k1.

Next row: (WS, CC) K1, *sl 1 wyf, p1; rep from * to last 2 sts, sl 1 wyf, k1.

Next row: (RS, MC) K2, *sl 1 wyb, k1; rep from * to last st, k1.

Next row: (WS, MC) K2, *sl 1 wyf, k1; rep from * to last st, k1.

Knit 2 rows with CC.

Knit 3 rows with MC.

Next row: (WS) BO all sts kwise.

Finishing

Weave in ends. Wet block to measurements (see page 34). Use blocking wires to help you obtain crisp, straight edges during the blocking process.

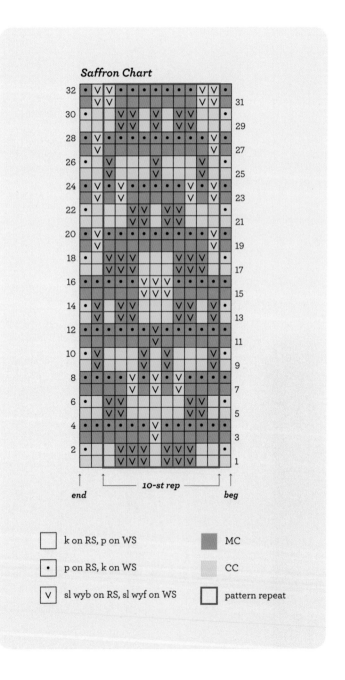

Saffron Chart

10-st rep

end   beg

k on RS, p on WS

• p on RS, k on WS

V sl wyb on RS, sl wyf on WS

MC

CC

pattern repeat

spark
sweater

////////////// Named for the small sparks in the centers of the star motifs, this yoked pullover will be a stunning showpiece of your stranded colorwork skills. Although it was designed to play with only two colors, this sweater is full of color possibility. Think of the variations you could create! Choose strongly contrasting colors for a bold effect or similar, monochromatic colors for a more subtle look. You could also choose a strong main color and fade the background with several lighter colors. This sweater will help you practice stranded knitting in the round and has the added bonus of providing practice with trapping floats of both colors.

Finished Size
36 (39¼, 42½, 49, 52¼, 55½)" (91.5 [99.5, 108, 124.5, 132.5, 141] cm) bust circumference.

Pullover shown measures 39¼" (99.5 cm); modeled with about 6" (15 cm) of positive ease.

Yarn
DK weight (#3 Light)

Shown in: Hedgehog Fibres Merino DK (100% superwash Merino wool; 218 yd [200 m]/4 oz

[115 g]): Urchin (MC), 3 (4, 4, 5, 5, 6); and Salty Tales (CC), 2 (3, 3, 3, 4, 4) skeins.

Needles
Size 1 (2.25 mm): 16" (40 cm) and 32" (80 cm) circular (cir) and set of 4 or 5 double-pointed (dpn).

Size 3 (3.25 mm): 16" (40 cm), 24" (60 cm), and 32" (80 cm) cir and set of 4 or 5 double-pointed (dpn).

Adjust needle size if necessary to obtain the correct gauge.

Notions
Markers (m); waste yarn; tapestry needle.

Gauge
24½ sts and 29 rnds = 4" (10 cm) in chart patt with larger needles; 24 sts and 30 rnds = 4" (10 cm) in St st with larger needles.

Notes
✚ This pullover is worked in the round from the top down with yoke shaping.

✚ The sleeves are worked in the round from the yoke down to the cuff.

Stitch Guide
Twisted Rib (multiple of 3 sts)
All rnds: *P2, k1-tbl; rep from * to end.

Body

With shorter smaller cir needle and CC, CO 117 (123, 129, 135, 138, 141) sts. Place marker (pm) and join in the rnd, taking care not to twist sts.

Work in Twisted Rib (see Stitch Guide) until collar measures 1½" (3.8 cm) from CO. Change to shortest larger cir needle.

Inc rnd: Knit and inc 3 (5, 7, 1, 6, 3) st(s) evenly spaced—120 (128, 136, 136, 144, 144) sts.

Knit 1 rnd even.

Inc rnd: *K2, M1L; rep from * to end—180 (192, 204, 204, 216, 216) sts. Change to 24" (60 cm)-long larger cir needle.

Knit 1 rnd even.

SHAPE NECK

Short-row 1: (RS) K35 (38, 36, 36, 39, 39), w&t.

Short-row 2: (WS) P70 (76, 72, 72, 78, 78), w&t.

✦ **Note:** For the remainder of the short-row shaping, work wraps together with their corresponding stitches whenever you come to them.

Short-row 3: Knit to 4 sts past last wrapped st, w&t.

Short-row 4: Purl to 4 sts past last wrapped st, w&t.

Rep last 2 short-rows 2 (2, 3, 4, 4, 4) more times.

Work rows 1–9 of Chart A.

With CC only, knit 3 rnds. Change to longest larger cir needle.

Inc rnd: *K3, M1L; rep from * to end—240 (256, 272, 272, 288, 288) sts.

Knit 3 rnds even.

Work rows 1–9 of Chart B, beg at arrow for your size.

With MC only, knit 1 rnd.

Inc rnd: *K4, M1L; rep from * to end—300 (320, 340, 340, 360, 360) sts.

Work rows 1–17 of Chart C, beg at arrow for your size.

Size 36" (91.5 cm) Only
With MC only, knit 2 rnds.

Sizes 39¼ (42½)" (99.5 [108] cm) Only
With MC only, knit 4 rnds, then work rows 1–7 (12) of Chart D.

Sizes 49 (52¼, 55½)" (124.5 [132.5, 141] cm) Only
With MC only, knit 1 rnd.

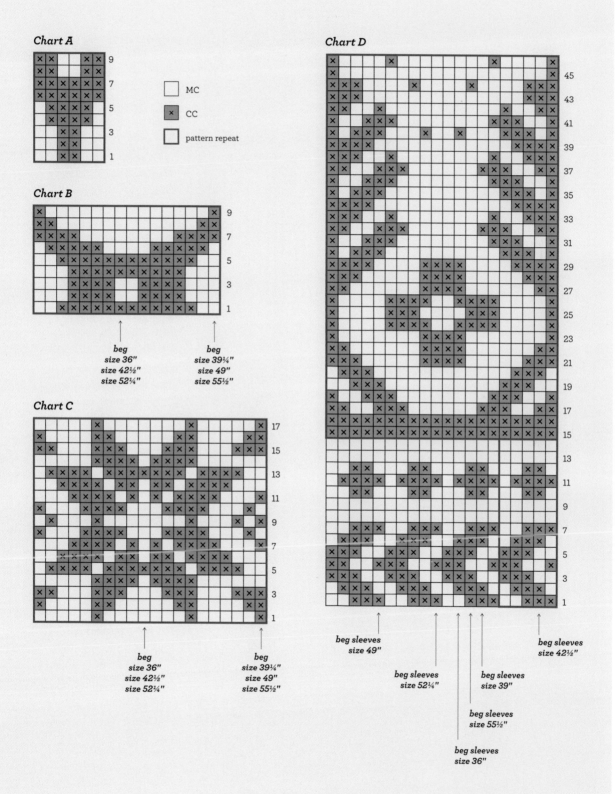

Chart A

Chart B

beg
size 36"
size 42½"
size 52¼"

beg
size 39¼"
size 49"
size 55½"

Chart C

beg
size 36"
size 42½"
size 52¼"

beg
size 39¼"
size 49"
size 55½"

Chart D

MC

CC

pattern repeat

beg sleeves
size 49"

beg sleeves
size 52¼"

beg sleeves
size 55½"

beg sleeves
size 39"

beg sleeves
size 42½"

beg sleeves
size 36"

Inc rnd: Knit and inc 70 (70, 90) sts evenly around—410 (430, 450) sts.

Knit 2 rnds even.

Work rnds 1–12 of Chart D.

All Sizes

Yoke should measure about 9¼ (10¼, 11¼, 11½, 11½, 11½)" (23.5 [26, 28.5, 29, 29] cm) from CO edge at center of back.

Divide Body and Sleeves

Next rnd: K48 (52, 54, 66, 69, 71) for half of back, place next 53 (54, 61, 73, 78, 82) sts on waste yarn for left sleeve, using Backward Loop method (see Glossary), CO 16 (18, 22, 22, 26, 28) sts for underarm, k97 (107, 109, 132, 135, 143) for front, place next 53 (54, 61, 73, 78, 82) sts on waste yarn for right sleeve, CO 16 (18, 22, 22, 26, 28) sts for underarm, then knit rem 49 (53, 55, 66, 70, 72) sts—226 (248, 262, 308, 326, 342) sts.

Dec rnd: Knit to beg-of-rnd m while dec 6 (8, 2, 8, 6, 2) sts evenly spaced, then knit 56 (61, 66, 76, 82, 85) more sts to center of underarm—220 (240, 260, 300, 320, 340) sts rem. Pm for new beg of rnd.

Work rnds 1–46 (10–46, 15–46, 15–46, 15–46, 15–46) of Chart D.

With MC only, knit 1 rnd and dec 4 (6, 5, 6, 8, 7) sts evenly spaced—216 (234, 255, 294, 312, 333) sts rem.

Cont even until piece measures 10¾ (10¾, 10¾, 11¼, 11¾, 12¼)" (27.5 [27.5, 27.5, 28.5, 30, 31] cm) from underarm.

Change to longer smaller cir needle.

Work 2¾" (7 cm) of Twisted Rib. BO all sts in patt.

Sleeves (make 2)

Return held 53 (54, 61, 73, 78, 82) sts to larger dpn.

With RS facing and MC, beg at center of underarm, pick up and knit 8 (9, 11, 11, 13, 14) sts along underarm CO, k53 (54, 61, 73, 78, 82) sleeve sts, pick up and knit 8 (9, 11, 11, 13, 14) sts along rem underarm CO—69 (72, 83, 95, 104, 110) sts. Pm and join in the rnd. Knit 2 rnds.

Next rnd: K2 with MC, working picked-up sts into chart patt, work rnd 1 (10, 15, 15, 15, 15) of Chart D as established to last 2 sts, k2 with MC.

Keeping first 2 sts and last 2 sts in MC only, beg at arrow for your size and work rnds 2–46 (10–46, 15–46, 15–46, 15–46, 15–46) of chart. (✦ *Note: For rows 15 and 16, slip the first 2 and last 2 sts of the rnd purlwise to keep them in MC.*) **At the same time,** when sleeve measures 1½" (3.8 cm) from underarm, beg shaping sleeve.

Dec rnd: (K1, ssk) in MC, work in next rnd of chart to last 3 sts, (k2tog, k1) in MC—2 sts dec'd.

Rep Dec rnd every 10 (10, 8, 6, 6, 4) rnds 4 (5, 5, 10, 7, 24) more times, then every 8 (8, 6, 4, 4, 0) rnds 7 (5, 10, 9, 15, 0) times—45 (50, 51, 55, 58, 60) sts rem. **At the same time**, when chart is complete, cont with MC only.

Work even until piece measures 15 (15, 15½, 15½, 16, 16)" (38 [38, 39.5, 39.5, 40.5, 40.5] cm) from underarm.

Knit 1 rnd and dec 0 (2, 0, 1, 1, 0) st(s) evenly spaced—45 (48, 51, 54, 57, 60) sts rem. Change to smaller dpn. Work 2" (5 cm) of Twisted Rib. BO all sts in patt.

Finishing

Weave in ends. Block to measurements (see page 34).

FRONT & BACK

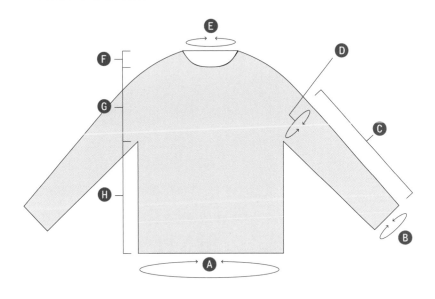

A: 36 (39¼, 42½, 49, 52¼, 55½)"
91.5 (99.5, 108, 124.5, 132.5, 141) cm

B: 7½ (8¼, 8½, 9¼, 9¾, 10)"
19 (21, 21.5, 23.5, 25, 25.5) cm

C: 17 (17, 17½, 17½, 18, 18)"
43 (43, 44.5, 44.5, 45.5, 45.5) cm

D: 11¼ (11¾, 13½, 15½, 17, 18)"
28.5 (30, 34.5, 39.5, 43, 45.5) cm

E: 19 (20, 21, 22, 22½, 23)"
48.5 (51, 53.5, 56, 57, 58.5) cm

F: 1 (1, 1¼, 1½, 1½, 1½)"
2.5 (2.5, 3.2, 3.8, 3.8, 3.8) cm

G: 8¼ (9¼, 10, 10¼, 10¼, 10¼)"
21 (23.5, 25.5, 26, 26, 26) cm

H: 13½ (13½, 13½, 14, 14½, 15)"
34.5 (34.5, 34.5, 35.5, 37, 38) cm

glossary /

These entries are listed alphabetically rather than grouped into categories. I give my abbreviation first, followed by the abbreviations you may see in other designers' patterns.

Backward Loop Increase—Left Leaning (BL-left)

Twist the yarn and place it on the right-hand needle **1** so that it matches the stitch in **2**. Take care to make sure the yarn tail is coming out in the correct position because this determines which way the increased stitch slants.

Brkyobrk (a 2-st increase)

Brioche knit into the next stitch **1**, leave the stitch on the needle, yarn over **2**, then brioche knit again into the same stitch **3**.

 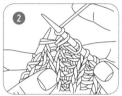

Backward Loop Increase—Right Leaning (BL-right)

Twist the yarn and place it on the right-hand needle so that it looks like the illustration. Take care to make sure the yarn tail is coming out in the correct position because this determines which way the increased stitch slants.

the right color combination can take a hat or sweater from a simple piece of clothing to an absolutely stunning, must-knit, must-have item.

Br4st Dec (a 4-st centered double decrease) (AKA brcdd)

Slip each of next 2 stitches knitwise 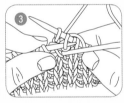, place the next stitch on a cable needle and hold it to the front . Knit the next stitch, then pass the second slipped stitch over the top 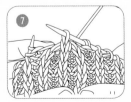. Slip the stitch back to the left-hand needle, pick up the next stitch, and pass it over 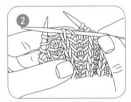. Slip the stitch back to the right-hand needle and pass the first slipped st over the top 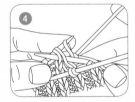. Return the stitch from the cable needle to the left-hand needle, then slip the stitch from the right-hand needle back on the left-hand needle. Pass the stitch from the cable needle over the other stitch 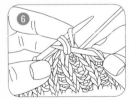. Slip the finished decrease stitch back to the right needle .

approx approximately

beg begin(ning)

BL–left backward loop increase—left leaning

BL–right backward loop increase—right leaning

BO bind off

Br4st brioche four-stitch

brk brioche knit

brkyobrk (brioche knit, yarn over, brioche knit) in the same stitch (increase)

brLsl brioche left slant (decrease)

brp brioche purl

brRsl brioche right slant (decrease)

CC contrast color

cir circular

cn cable needle

CO cast on

cont continue(s); continuing

DC dark color

dec('d) decrease(s); decreasing; decreased

DK double knit(ting)

dpn double-pointed needle(s)

DS dark side

DSP double stitch pair

foll follow(s); following

inc('d) increase(s); increasing; increased

k knit

k1f&b knit into the front and back of the same stitch

k2tog knit two together

kwise knitwise

LC light color

LH left-hand

LLI left lifted increase

LS light side

m marker

M1L make 1 (left slant)

M1R make 1 (right slant)

MC main color

p purl

p1f&b purl into the front and back of the same stitch

p2tog purl two together

patt(s) pattern(s)

pm place marker

rem remain(ing)

rep repeat

RH right-hand

RLI right lifted increase

rnd(s) round(s)

RS right side

sl slip

sl1yo slip one yarn over

sm slip marker

ssk slip, slip, knit (decrease)

ssp slip, slip, purl (decrease)

St st stockinette stitch

st(s) stitch(es)

tbl through back loop(s)

tog together

w&t wrap and turn

WS wrong side

wyb with yarn in back

wyf with yarn in front

yo yarn over

Br4st Inc (a 4-st increase) *(AKA brkyobrkyobrk)*

Brk into the next stitch, leave the stitch on the needle while you create a yo, then brk again, create another yo and brk one last time into the same stitch.

Brioche Left Slant (a 2-stitch left leaning decrease) (BrLsl) *(AKA bsk2p or brssk)*

Slip the first stitch knitwise ❶, brioche knit the next 2 stitches together ❷, then pass the slipped stitch over ❸.

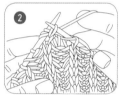

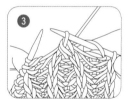

Brioche Knit (Brk)

Knit the slipped stitch together with its accompanying yarn over.

Brioche Purl (Brp)

Purl the slipped stitch together with its accompanying yarn over.

Brioche Right Slant (a 2-stitch right leaning decrease) (BrRsl) *(AKA brk2tog)*

Slip the first stitch knitwise, knit the next stitch ❶, then pass the slipped stitch over ❷. Slip the decrease stitch back to the left-hand needle, then lift the next stitch and pass it over the first ❸. Return decrease stitch to right-hand needle ❹.

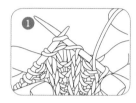

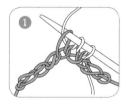

Crochet Provisional Cast-On

With waste yarn and crochet hook, make a loose crochet chain about 4 stitches longer than you need to cast on. With knitting needle, working yarn, and beginning 2 stitches from right end of chain, pick up and knit 1 stitch through the back loop of each crochet chain ❶ for the desired number of stitches. When you're ready to work in the opposite direction, pull out the crochet chain to expose the live stitches ❷.

Crochet Chain

Make a slipknot and place it on the crochet hook. *Yarn over hook and draw through the loop on the hook. Repeat from * for the desired number of stitches (shown in the illustration). To fasten off, cut yarn and draw end through last loop formed.

DK Decrease Left Slanting

Rearrange the 2 DSPs involved in the decrease so that the 2 light stitches and the 2 dark stitches are positioned next to each other ❶. With both yarns in the back, use the light color to knit the 2 light stitches together ❷, move both yarns to the front and use the dark color to ssp the dark stitches together ❸. Remember to move both yarns to the back before continuing.

I-cord

With double-pointed needle, cast on the desired number of stitches. *Without turning the needle, slide the stitches to other end of the needle, pull the yarn around the back, and knit the stitches as usual; repeat from * for desired length.

Italian Two-Color Cast-On

Use a slipknot to tie the two colors together and place it on right needle (this stitch does not count in the cast-on and will later be unraveled). Insert your left thumb and index finger between two strands, with the contrast color over the thumb ❶. To create the knit stitch, bring needle toward you, under front strand, up between strands, over back strand to grab it and pull it under front strand to make loop on needle ❷. To create the next purl stitch, take needle away from you, over both strands, under both strands, up to grab front strand and pull it under back strand to make loop on needle ❸. Continue alternating knit and purl stitches, ending with a knit stitch. Turn work. Keeping strands crossed to preserve the last cast-on stitch, work 1 row as foll: *p1, k1; rep from * to end.

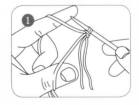

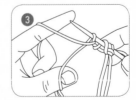

Italian Two-Color Bind-Off

Cut yarn, leaving a tail at least three times longer than the edge to be bound off. When worked on plain ribbing, every stitch will be worked through a single stitch loop. When worked on brioche, treat yarn-over wraps as part of the companion knit or purl stitch.

1. Insert the tapestry needle purlwise into the first knit loop on the knitting needle ❶. Draw through, then wrap around side of fabric (not over needle) to the back.

2. From the back, insert tapestry needle knitwise into the first purl loop (the second loop on knitting needle) and draw it through ❷.

3. Insert the tapestry needle into first knit loop knitwise, slip the loop off the knitting needle and onto the tapestry needle. Insert the tapestry needle purlwise into the second knit stitch (now the second loop on the knitting needle). Draw the yarn through ❸.

4. Insert the tapestry needle into the first purl loop purlwise, slip the loop off the knitting needle onto the tapestry needle. Wrap the tapestry needle to the back of the work, then insert knitwise into the second purl loop (now the second loop on knitting needle). Draw the yarn through ❹. Repeat steps 3 and 4.

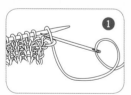
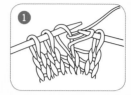
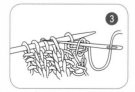

Knit 1 Stitch, Front & Back (K1f&b)

Knit into a stitch and leave it on the needle ❶. Knit through the back loop of the same stitch ❷. Slip both stitches off the needle ❸.

Kitchener Stitch

1. Bring threaded needle through front stitch as if to purl and leave stitch on needle ❶.

2. Bring threaded needle through back stitch as if to knit and leave stitch on needle ❷.

3. Bring threaded needle through first front stitch as if to knit and slip this stitch off needle. Bring threaded needle through next front stitch as if to purl and leave stitch on needle ❸.

4. Bring threaded needle through first back stitch as if to purl and slip this stitch off needle. Bring needle through next back stitch as if to knit and leave stitch on needle ❹. Repeat steps 3 and 4 until no stitches remain on needles.

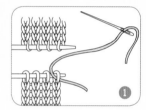
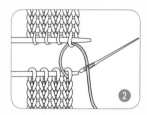
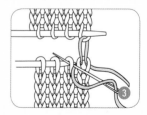
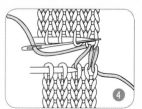

Left Lifted Increase (LLI)

Insert the tip of the left needle from back to front into the stitch 2 rows below the stitch on the right needle ❶. Knit this stitch through the back loop ❷.

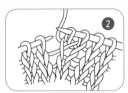

Mattress Stitch Seam

With RS of knitting facing, use threaded needle to pick up one bar between first 2 stitches on one piece, then cor-

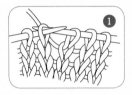

responding bar plus the bar above it on other piece. *Pick up next 2 bars on first piece, then next 2 bars on other. Repeat from * to end of seam, finishing by picking up last bar (or pair of bars) at the top of first piece.

Make One (Left Slant) (M1L)

With left needle tip, lift strand between needles from front to back ❶. Knit lifted loop through the back ❷.

Make One (Right Slant) (M1R)

With left needle tip, lift strand between needles from back to front ❶. Knit lifted loop through the front ❷.

Right Lifted Increase (RLI)

Insert the tip of the right needle from back to front into the stitch

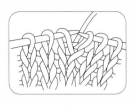

in the row below the next stitch on the left needle and lift this stitch onto the left needle, then knit into it (see illustration).

Short-Rows (Knit Side)

Work to turning point, slip next stitch purlwise ❶, bring the yarn to the front, then slip the same stitch back to the left needle ❷, turn the work around and bring the yarn in position for the next stitch—1 stitch has been wrapped and the yarn is correctly positioned to work the next stitch. When you come to a wrapped stitch on a subsequent knit row, hide the wrap by working it together with the wrapped stitch as follows: Insert right needle tip under the wrap from the front ❸, then into the stitch on the needle, and work the stitch and its wrap together as a single stitch.

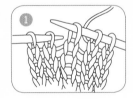

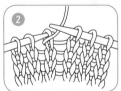

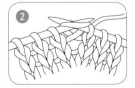

Short-Rows (Purl Side)

Work to the turning point, slip the next stitch purlwise to the right needle, bring the yarn to the back of the work 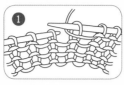, return the slipped stitch to the left needle, bring the yarn to the front between the needles 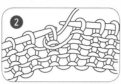, and turn the work so that the knit side is facing—1 stitch has been wrapped and the yarn is correctly positioned to knit the next stitch. To hide the wrap on a subsequent purl row, work to the wrapped stitch, use the tip of the right needle to pick up the wrap from the back, place it on the left needle 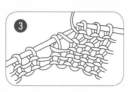, then purl it together with the wrapped stitch.

Sl1yo

A term used in brioche knitting to indicate slip 1 stitch and create a yarn over. To work, always bring the yarn in front, slip the next stitch purlwise, then bring the yarn over the top of the slipped stitch, creating a yarn over that lies over the top of the slipped stitch.

Slip Slip Knit (Ssk)

Slip 2 stitches knitwise one at a time 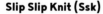. Insert point of left needle into front of 2 slipped stitches and knit them together through back loops with right needle 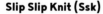.

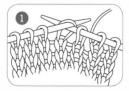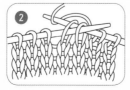

Slip Slip Purl (Ssp)

Holding yarn in front, slip 2 stitches knitwise one at a time onto right needle 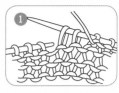. Slip them back onto left needle and purl the 2 stitches together through back loops 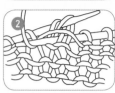.

Three-Needle Bind-Off

Place the stitches to be joined onto 2 separate needles and hold the needles parallel so that the right sides of knitting face together. Insert a third needle into the first stitch on each of 2 needles 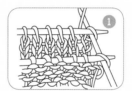 and knit them together as 1 stitch 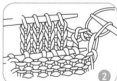, *knit the next stitch on each needle the same way, then use the left needle tip to lift the first stitch over the second and off the needle 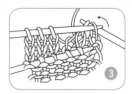. Repeat from * until no stitches remain on first 2 needles. Cut yarn and pull tail through last stitch to secure.

Yarn Over (yo)

Wrap the yarn around the needle from front to back.

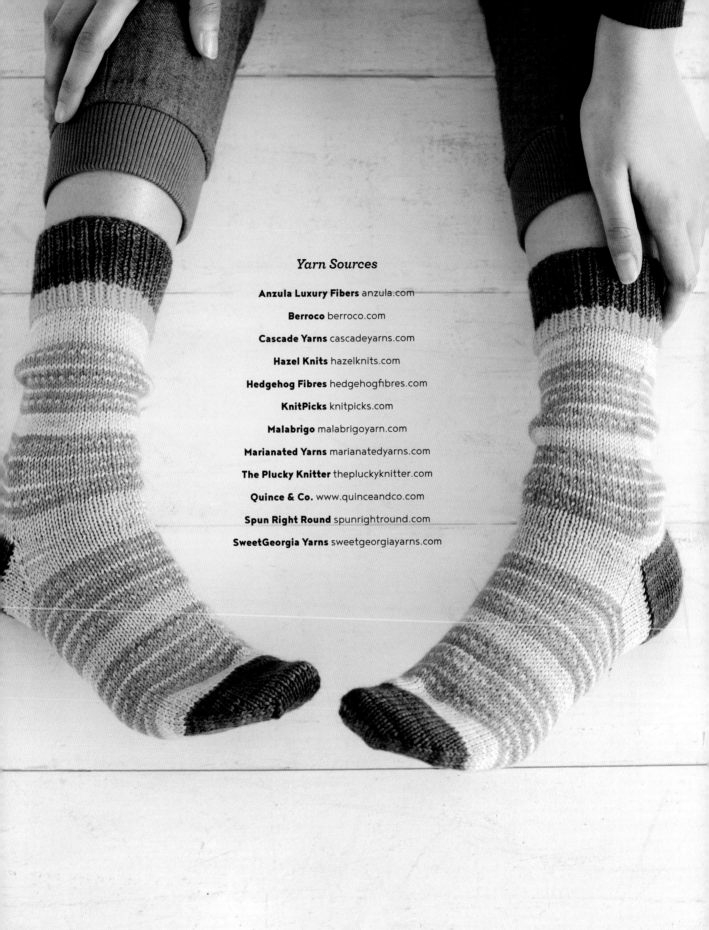

Yarn Sources

Anzula Luxury Fibers anzula.com

Berroco berroco.com

Cascade Yarns cascadeyarns.com

Hazel Knits hazelknits.com

Hedgehog Fibres hedgehogfibres.com

KnitPicks knitpicks.com

Malabrigo malabrigoyarn.com

Marianated Yarns marianatedyarns.com

The Plucky Knitter thepluckyknitter.com

Quince & Co. www.quinceandco.com

Spun Right Round spunrightround.com

SweetGeorgia Yarns sweetgeorgiayarns.com

acknowledgments

It truly takes a village to write a book. This process has been a crazy ride from the beginning, and it would not have been possible without the following people:

To my editors, Kerry and Nathalie, thank you for entrusting me with this undertaking and for holding my hand along the way. To my technical editor, Therese, thanks for working your magic on my patterns.

Thank you to my amazing test knitters and their attention to detail and helpful suggestions.

To Hayley, thanks for making all the yarn magic happen (again and again and again!). Speaking of yarn magic, a gigantic, larger-than-life thank-you to all of the yarn companies and indie dyers that generously provided yarn for this book and made it look so beautiful.

Thank you to Lisa, Sarah, and Mary for being my hive mind and moral support unit!

To Megan and Katie, thanks for being my biggest fans and giving the best pep talks!

Thank you to my parents for being my cheerleaders and to the rest of my family for bravely wearing some of my early creations. Also, a special shout-out to my mom for being a courageous sock sample knitter!

Most of all, thanks to my husband, Nate, for being my sounding board, in-house editor, and untiring ear throughout this last year—for buying me a lot of Cherry Garcia ice cream, organizing numerous "boys' nights" with our kids, and overall making this book happen! I love you!

ABOUT THE AUTHOR

Jesie Ostermiller is an avid self-taught knitter and designer with a passion for colorwork. Her designs have been featured in various Interweave publications and can be found on Ravelry. She was born and raised in Alaska, and it was there that she fell in love with knitting cold-weather necessities such as sweaters, hats, mittens, and scarves. She now lives in northern Utah with her husband and two boys, which thankfully still affords her plenty of winter weather in which to wear her knitted creations.

Photo: Kate Ryskamp

index